GOD'S
MANY-SPLENDORED
IMAGE

God's Many-Splendored Image

Theological Anthropology for Christian Formation

Nonna Verna Harrison

Baker Academic
a division of Baker Publishing Group
Grand Rapids, Michigan

© 2010 by Nonna Verna Harrison

Published by Baker Academic
a division of Baker Publishing Group
P.O. Box 6287, Grand Rapids, MI 49516-6287
www.bakeracademic.com

Printed in the United States of America

Library of Congress Cataloging-in-Publication Data
Harrison, Verna E. F.
    God's many-splendored image : theological anthropology for Christian formation / Nonna Verna Harrison.
        p.   cm.
    Includes bibliographical references and index.
    ISBN 978-0-8010-3471-8 (pbk.)
    1. Christian life. 2. Image of God. 3. Fathers of the church. I. Title.
BV4501.3.H368 2010
248.4—dc22   2009049425

This book is dedicated to all those people
whom other people have thrown away.
It shows that God does not throw away people.

Contents

Foreword

What does it mean to be human? That is the question Sister Nonna sets out to answer in this present work. It is an all-important question. And, as she emphasizes, it is not a simple question to answer. Who am I? What am I? None of us can easily say. The bounds of human personhood are exceedingly wide ranging, reaching out of space into infinity and out of time to eternity. In the words of the Bible, "The heart is deep" (Ps. 64:6). As Sister Nonna affirms in her conclusion, "Human identity is an unfathomable depth of mystery. . . . There is always more waiting to be discovered and a further mystery that remains beyond our grasp. We are on a journey of discovery that has no end."

The present book provides us with invaluable guidance on this exploratory journey. Sister Nonna writes as an expert in the early Christian world and its literature, but she presents the fruits of her learning in a form that is readily accessible to every reader. Her style is simple yet profound, vivid yet never overstated. The book is enhanced by many striking quotations, especially from the Sayings of the Desert Fathers, but she also draws on more-modern material, on George MacDonald and Martin Luther King as well as St. Gregory of Nyssa, on Kepler and Einstein as well as St. Maximus the Confessor. I was particularly interested in what she has to say about the status of women and about artistic creativity and in her treatment of our human relationship to the animals. Here she speaks in generous and compassionate terms, yet without sentimentality.

Sister Nonna rightly underlines the uniqueness of each human person. We are all created in the image of God, and yet we each realize that image in our own distinctive way; this is because every human being is endowed with freedom of choice. Personal freedom and uniqueness are two of the master themes of this book, and as I read it I often called to mind two Jewish sayings recorded by Martin Buber in *The Tales of the Hasidim*: God never does the same thing twice, and the world has need of every single human being. Sister Nonna confronts the difficult issue of why, if early Christianity attached such value to freedom, it did not more firmly oppose the institution of slavery. She provides a better answer than I have found elsewhere.

The author sums up the basic message of her work in the words, "This book aims to show readers that all people have value before God." She has indeed succeeded in achieving this objective. And her message is altogether timely, for we live in an era when—in the Western world, at any rate—among all too many people there is a tragic loss of meaning and hope. As somebody said to me recently, "If I died tomorrow, nobody would notice." This book is an honest and effective response to such despondency. On reaching the final page, I was led to exclaim with the psalmist, "I will give thanks unto Thee for I am fearfully and wonderfully made" (Ps. 139:14). Here truly is a work that I can recommend with all my heart.

+ Metropolitan Kallistos (Ware) of Diokleia

Acknowledgments

This book summarizes much of what I have learned about patristic theological anthropology in more than thirty years of study. I am appreciative of conversations with many teachers and colleagues with whom I have worked throughout this time and for their encouragement. In particular, I would like to thank Dean Pamela Couture of Saint Paul School of Theology, who challenged me to write this book. I appreciate the way she and all my faculty colleagues at Saint Paul carried the burden of extra work so that I could spend a sabbatical writing this manuscript during spring semester 2008.

Let me also thank Dean John Behr of St. Vladimir's Orthodox Theological Seminary for taking time from a very busy schedule to check my reworkings of three texts of his translation of Irenaeus from the Armenian, a language I do not know.

In fall 2008, I attended a dinner with faculty and trustees at Saint Paul. The after-dinner speaker quoted Albert Einstein as commending "holy curiosity." I asked John Oyler, the public services librarian at Saint Paul, to find the source of the quote. To my astonishment, he found it in the middle of a six-hundred-page biography of Einstein. He also supplied me with a number of other books on the famous Jewish physicist. This material became the nucleus of chapter 8 of this book. I am thankful for

John's help in this and in many other ways. I am also thankful to my friend and academic comrade-in-arms Sherry Wright for much encouragement and for the quote from Martin Luther King Jr. that graces the beginning of chapter 5.

Finally, let me thank James Ernest, my editor at Baker Academic, for gentle guidance in the process of turning my idea into a book.

Teaching and research always take place in a community. We listen to, read, and learn from others; we cite them in appreciation; we write and present papers to share our work with others; we are corrected by them; and the conversation among many voices continues. I would like to thank those who have contributed to this book but whose names I have not remembered to mention here. Whatever errors remain in it are, of course, my own.

Sr. Nonna Verna Harrison
May 13, 2009

Introduction

As I was growing up, I asked myself many questions about who I was as a human person. During my teenage years I saw a science fiction program on television that questioned the meaning of human existence in a way I found particularly troubling. The story is set some time in the near future when the earth is overpopulated and lacks the resources to support so many people. An "ethical suicide" program is in place to help deal with this problem. Volunteers who want to help reduce the population are invited to come to a quiet, spacious, comfortably furnished room and talk with friendly staff while they are served their favorite meal. After this they are given a lethal injection. The film shows a man who has chosen to go through this process. At the end, as he and the friendly woman staffer with a soothing voice are in conversation, a doctor in a lab coat comes in and gives him the injection. He asks if he can ask one more question. As the woman says yes, the doctor whispers in her ear that she will not have time to answer it. Then the volunteer asks, "What are people for?" Just then his head falls to one side and he dies. After the program ended, I thought to myself that human life must have more meaning and purpose than that, but I was unable to articulate what the meaning and purpose might be.

Today the world is much more overpopulated than it was then, and resources have become even more scarce. We live in

1

an age of depersonalization that calls into question the value of each person's individual existence. In industrialized countries, government agencies and large corporations use computer databases to keep track of everyone. Most telephone calls lead to machines instead of people. We are treated like arbitrary numbers instead of unique, unrepeatable human beings, and a random keystroke error can ruin someone's life. In developing countries, conditions are far worse for all but the wealthy few. Random acts of terrorism target large groups of civilians in order to attract worldwide publicity. Wars, pandemics, and natural disasters wipe out people a thousand at a time. In parts of Asia and Eastern Europe, young women and children are forced into slavery and used as prostitutes until they die at a young age from AIDS or other causes. Sometimes desperately poor parents will sell a daughter into this kind of involuntary servitude in order to feed several other children. In today's world, people with resources are treated as consumers from whom the powerful can extract money; people with no resources are often treated as disposable commodities to be consumed. It should come as no surprise, then, that now more than ever many wonder what people are really for.

This book starts from my childhood questions about what it is to be human. At age twenty, I became a Christian and discovered that God provides the foundation, meaning, and purpose of life for each individual and community and for humankind as a whole. In adulthood I have studied, taught, and researched early Christian theology and the Eastern Christian theology that has built on its ancient foundations. Over more than a quarter of a century I have continued to ask questions about human identity. I have pursued these questions through research and have found many answers in early Christian writings. Although the fruits of my studies have been published in specialized books and scholarly articles, I am aware that many people beyond the world of academia have the same kinds of questions about being human that I have asked myself. This book invites them to join me in asking these questions and in discovering illuminating answers in the Christian theological heritage.

The difficulty is that folks today frequently see a Christian understanding of human identity as part of the problem. This is because an oversimplified negative vision of humanity is taken for granted in popular culture, and churches often reflect this negative vision without even thinking about it. An example will show how this happens. Let's say there is a big financial scandal in Washington, DC. Solid evidence shows that members of congress and presidents of large corporations have fraudulently stolen public money for personal use. Commentators in the newspapers and on television explain that the fraud occurred because people are greedy, and greed is human nature. Without thinking, folks routinely identify "human nature" as the cause of weakness, error, and ethical lapses and as the source of all the world's troubles. So is it true that weakness, error, and ethical lapses due to greed, envy, and malice are at the core of what we and our neighbors really are as human beings? How then can we still affirm our human dignity or the human dignity of others?

This negative attitude toward human nature is often unconscious, but it pervades our culture. Combined with the ever-present pressures of depersonalization, it is enough to drive people to cynicism and despair. It leaves many in deep emotional and spiritual pain. When young people cannot find value and hope in their lives, they may turn to drugs, high risk relationships, violence, or other self-destructive activities.

When those troubled by questions about who they are step into a church, where they can reasonably expect to find healing, the same negative message is often repeated. For example, the preacher may talk about the financial scandal from the pulpit and conclude that since greed is human nature, we are all greedy and need to ask God for forgiveness. We have to condemn ourselves and turn to God. The negative message of secular pop culture is repeated in Christian pop culture, but now it is presented in the name of God and supposedly with divine authority. Such a message cannot heal the pain of depersonalization and the lost sense of human dignity; it only makes the person seeking Christ's healing word feel misunderstood and even more hurt.

Are Christians echoing the toxic messages of today's ailing culture without realizing it? Is the medicine churches offer to heal the wounds actually making them worse? The message that takes aim at corrupt "human nature" from the pulpit may actually derive from a toxic assumption of secular culture that has seeped imperceptibly into the community of faith. Such negative preaching may also reflect a narrow, oversimplified vision of humanity that has long been familiar in both Protestant and Catholic theologies. Yet regardless of where in history the negative view of human nature originated, today many Christians as well as non-Christians find it unacceptable. Many outside the church think Christianity teaches that human beings are inherently bad and guilty and that human freedom is dangerous and gets us into trouble. Many inside the church fear they might be right.

One of my students at Saint Paul School of Theology wrote in a paper, "The problem with human beings is that they are just too human," and, "Humans have become too human, i.e., fallen short of the image of God." Another student wrote that sanctification is "the struggle between human nature and the image of God within the individual." My students probably did not stop to think about what these statements imply. They raise hard questions. Is what I am as a human being fundamentally bad? Do I have to reject my own inherent identity in order to become acceptable to God? Is God opposed to me because of who I am? If God created me in his own image, how can what I am be opposed to God? Is it even possible to love such a God?

Because of the psychological, social, and cultural pressures that beset people today, many secretly fear they are so evil inside that they can never do good for others or become the good persons they long to be. How can they hear the good news of the gospel if Christianity only confirms their worst fears about who they are? And how can pastors explain what we are as human beings in a way that can free them from this fear? Surely the good news is that God created us with an inherent capacity for goodness, and Christ can help us, little by little, to learn to do good for others so that over time and with the help of divine grace we can become good.

The popular idea that Christianity says "human nature" is inherently bad is actually the opposite of what the earliest Christian theologians believed. This book challenges the popularized negative view by proposing a prophetic alternative grounded in early Greek Christian sources. It draws on the wealth of early theological reflection, the wisdom of the desert mothers and fathers, and the heritage of Eastern Christianity to discover what God has made us to be.

Throughout the ages, Christians have believed that the image of God in which we are created (Gen. 1:26–27) is at the core of who we are and defines us as human. Theologians and spiritual writers have found the divine image in many different aspects of what we are, what we can and should do, and what we are called to become. These aspects include freedom, spiritual perception, connectedness to God, virtues, royal dignity, a vital connection to the natural world, reason, creativity, personal uniqueness, community, mystery, and life. This book will make the case that the divine image is present not simply in one or two of these aspects of human identity but in all of them. They are many facets of the splendid jewel that each human person can become. God invites us to remove the dirt hiding these facets and polish them until they shine with the beauty God bestows on each of us.

Throughout the book we will listen to the prophetic voices of the early and Eastern Christian traditions that proclaim the true value and dignity of every human person and call us back to our authentic identity and purpose. Each chapter of this book explores a different facet of the divine image and likeness and maps out a path that can lead toward wholeness and holiness. We will begin each chapter with one of my childhood questions about human identity and a story that illustrates the question and begins to point toward an answer. Then we will explore early Christian writers, ideas, and stories that flesh out the answer. Each chapter describes a set of gifts included in the divine image and likeness and shows both how they can be used and developed rightly and how they can be misused. Each chapter includes practical suggestions about how we can learn to turn away from past mistakes, become as God really intends us to be, and participate in God's loving work in the world. We will see how our Creator has shared with us many gifts and powers so we can take part in God's creative work and collaborate in furthering his loving purposes for the world. Yet we will also see how our human gifts and powers are often distorted and misused when we separate ourselves from God and pursue goals that conflict with the harmony and flourishing of our neighbors, ourselves, and the whole of creation. Misuse of the gifts God has given us in the divine image has had devastating consequences. The resulting damage, however, does not express our authentic human nature. Rather, it reflects the ways that wrong choices by ourselves, others, and society as a whole have buried, wounded, or distorted our true nature. Nevertheless, the image of God remains present in us as a foundation and a potential that awaits our discovery and can transform our lives.

Early Christian reflection on the image of God shows what we have always been, what we can and should do now, and what we are called to become in the future. Some features of the divine image are already given to us at our creation, such as rationality, freedom, and the capacity for growth in virtue and communion with God. By freely collaborating with God's grace, we are to grow little by little throughout our lifetime into other features of the divine image, such as the practice of virtue, spiritual perception, and loving communion with God. Yet we hope for perfection in virtue, immortality, eternal growth in communion with God, and fuller participation in divine life as gifts that will be actualized only in the age to come. Life according to God's image thus combines a stable foundation with a dynamic movement that begins here and now but will continue beyond this life. As human beings we are called to an unending process of becoming more and more like God, especially by sharing God's character and God's love. Some early Christian and Eastern Christian theologians have described this process in terms of a distinction between the divine image and the divine likeness in Genesis 1:26. The "image" names the stable foundation in human nature that provides the potential for growth in likeness to God, communion with God, and collaboration in God's creative and loving activities. The dynamic movement into greater and greater actualization of this potential is called the divine "likeness." This distinction is a helpful shorthand, and though not all the theologians we will be studying use it, we will employ it in this book.

Although the fundamental purpose God has given to humankind is common to every human being, each is called to live out that purpose in a unique way. We can start from many diverse places and pursue different vocations and spiritual practices as we move toward a common goal in God's kingdom. We can start by pursuing a facet of the divine likeness that comes most naturally to us, with God's grace and calling, and in the process of pursuing it we will acquire other facets as well.

Each chapter of this book will focus on a different facet of God's image and likeness. Chapter 1 explores human freedom and responsibility. God has created us with freedom similar to God's own freedom so that we can spontaneously choose to love our Creator, who has first loved us. We can choose freely what we will become and what we will do. So we can choose either good or evil, and our choices have enormous consequences.

Chapter 2 explains how God, or Christ, is the model and we are the images. So as humans we have a connection to God at the very core of our being. When we separated ourselves from God through sin, Christ came to restore that connection, that is, to remake us in God's image and likeness. So now Christ incarnate is the model to follow, and he gives us the strength to come with him and finally reach eternal communion with God.

Chapter 3 is about the human capacity for spiritual perception, which is often hidden in our fallen world. It enables us to truly know, and therefore love, God and our fellow humans.

Chapter 4 is about the moral excellence of God, which also becomes the core of human likeness to God. There are many forms of moral excellence, or many virtues, and we can begin by pursuing the one that appeals to us, but we can hope, with God's help, eventually to acquire all of them. In order to do so, we have to learn humility along the way, as a foundation for working with God to do great things.

Chapters 5 through 9 address the great tasks that being God's image both enables and calls us to undertake in cooperation with God. Chapter 5 is about the royal dignity that all humans possess as images of God and about our task of treating others with genuine respect, especially those that society perceives as least valuable. Chapter 6 is concerned with the human body, which God made to work together with the soul to show forth his likeness here and now. Chapter 7 explores our divine calling to mediate God's presence in and care for the ecosystem in which we live, and for the whole of creation. Chapter 8 is about how God invites people to disclose divine beauty, wisdom, and providence through the arts and sciences. Chapter 9 examines how humankind, as a community, can come to participate in the divine community of the Holy Trinity and share with one another the same kind of mutual love the Father, Son, and Holy Spirit share.

Finally, in the conclusion, as we draw together our discussion of the different facets of the divine image, we will consider that there is far more than can be said in this book. The divine image is also an image of God's incomprehensibility. There is always more about humans—about our neighbors and ourselves—that is yet to be discovered.

1

Freedom

In the world today, we all value our freedom, and we declare to the world that we are free. Yet we also find we need to struggle for our freedom. Beneath our declarations, we may have anxious questions that we hesitate to reveal: Am I really free? What real choices do I have? Are there limits to my freedom? Freedom seems to be an end in itself, but, even if I have a million choices, what is the purpose of being free?

Basil of Caesarea, a fourth-century bishop in Cappadocia, or in what is now central Turkey, asked himself questions like these. He wondered about how much freedom people really have and how best to use that freedom. He came from a wealthy, aristocratic family in a world where many people were slaves and slavery was taken for granted as part of the social and economic system. Slavery was part of the only world people in Basil's time knew. In light of this, he tells the following story: Suppose there is an upright man who lives a good and disciplined life but is a slave. This man sees that his master is enslaved to the pleasures of a prostitute, though he himself dismisses her from his mind. Basil tells us he would say to that good man, "Know that you are a slave in name only. He," that is, the owner, "has the name of master, but he has established his slavery by deed."[1] My house in Kansas City is more than one hundred years old. There is a small room that opens into my bedroom with no door in between. I keep bookshelves and an exercise bike in it, but I am told that in the old days a servant would have lived there. From there he or she could see everything that went on in the master bedroom. In the ancient Mediterranean world, most people were poor, and a whole family would live in one room; but the rich lived in large houses surrounded by their servants. It is no wonder, then, that people went out into the desert to became monks or nuns; there they found the privacy they needed to live a life of prayer. The master in Basil's story would probably have slept on a bed, while his slave slept on the floor beside him. The slave could very easily have seen what Basil describes.

So Basil asks, which one is more free? The master's mind is filled with obsessive thoughts and fantasies about the prostitute. These thoughts, and the feelings that accompany them, drive his actions. He does not consider his wife and family, nor does he consider his reputation, which would have been very important to an aristocrat in the ancient world. He may be locked into the routine of a long-standing habit. So he is not free to use his reason to weigh the alternatives and make a sensible choice. He is addicted, or, in Basil's language, enslaved.

By contrast, the slave who witnesses his master's situation is free in mind and heart. He can dismiss from his mind the thought of the prostitute and any fantasies of pleasure that come with it. He has work to do, and since he cannot change his situation, he strives to do it out of love for his master and without resentment. In the ancient world, people did not know about different societies with different social structures, as they do today, so they did not envision the possibility of abolishing slavery, as Christian abolitionists did in the nineteenth century. Fourth-century Christians made use of the circumstances in

---

1. *On the Origin of Humanity* 1.8; trans. Harrison, *St. Basil*, 37.

which they found themselves to discover ways to love and serve God and their neighbors. While the slave's life was hard, it was simple; he had no alternative. He probably worked with his hands, leaving his mind free to pray. Basil's brother, the mystic and theologian Gregory of Nyssa, uses the concept of the divine image found in Genesis 1:26–27 to critique the whole idea of slavery. We will see what he says when we discuss the issue further in chapter 5. Social justice is important but so is inner freedom, the concern of this chapter. Inner freedom is the freedom of mind and heart. It is the ability to reason and make choices without constraint, including choices about the thoughts, emotions, attitudes, and drives that fill the inner landscape of oneself. Regardless of outward circumstances, everyone can work on developing this inner freedom. It is an important aspect of being human, and no oppressor can take it away. So the slave in Basil's story could cultivate it, while his undisciplined master chose not to do so.

The Importance of Freedom

Like people today, those in ancient times wondered whether they had real freedom of choice. Some believed that what people do is determined not by themselves but by chance, by fate, or by the stars. Some believed that things happen through the random collisions of atoms. Some held that fate, or the will of God, determines what will happen before people have an opportunity to choose. And, as happens today, some believed in astrology, which says that the movements of the stars govern how people will act and what will become of them. Yet for centuries many Greek philosophers affirmed human freedom. This is because philosophers greatly valued human reason and virtue, and they understood that without freedom, human reason would be powerless and ethical judgments would be senseless. After all, how could we praise good actions and blame evil ones if people were robots or puppets or if what they did happened simply by chance? The same question arises in today's American judicial system. Defendants who are considered insane, that is, incapable of making a free choice about their actions, are not considered guilty. But these are exceptional cases; everyone else is considered to be responsible for what he or she does.

Like the philosophers, ancient Christians found it very important to affirm human freedom of choice. Origen, a third-century student of Platonic philosophy who was also a great biblical scholar, affirms free choice as follows: "The teaching of the church includes the doctrine of the righteous judgment of God, a doctrine which, if believed to be true, summons its hearers to live a good life and by every means to avoid sin—for it assumes that they acknowledge that deeds worthy of praise or of blame lie within our own power."[2]

As Origen acknowledges, from the beginning the church taught that people are free. He suggests two important reasons for this teaching. First, God is just. If people were not free and God created them, God would be responsible for their sins and for all the evils of the fallen world. So Christians have to believe in human freedom in order to affirm God's goodness and justice. Second, God will judge people for their good or evil conduct, granting them eternal life in heaven or eternal punishment in hell based on how they have chosen to live on earth. If people were not inherently responsible for their actions, such a judgment would be unjust and make no sense. And in this world, the church could not make ethical judgments. If people could not make choices, pastors could not exhort them to do good or counsel them not to do evil. Thus the whole present life of the church presupposes human freedom, as does Christian hope for the age to come.

Indeed, the whole biblical story of the relationship of God with God's people presupposes human freedom. Through Moses and the prophets and in Jesus himself, God exhorts people to do good and warns them not to do evil. Origen quotes the following texts, among others, in support of human freedom:[3]

2. *On First Principles* 3.1.1; trans. Butterworth, *Origen*, 157.
3. *On First Principles* 3.1.6; trans. Butterworth, *Origen*, 164–65.

And what does the LORD require of you but to do justice, and to love kindness, and to walk humbly with your God? (Mic. 6:8)

See, I have set before you this day life and good, death and evil. . . . Therefore choose life. (Deut. 30:15, 19)

Every one then who hears these words of mine and does them will be like a wise man who built his house upon the rock. (Matt. 7:24)

Such words can only benefit people because they are free to choose how to live. When people today hear Scriptures like these and take them to heart, the concrete choices they make about how to treat their neighbors or how to spend their time will be different from what they would otherwise have been.

Freedom and the Image of God

Freedom is so important to living a Christian life, and so central to who we are as human beings, that the fourth-century Cappadocian Gregory of Nyssa considered it an important facet of the divine image that defines us as human. Gregory spent most of his life in the little town of Nyssa, where he had been sent as bishop. He served as pastor there but also wrote. His profound writings, which are of great interest today, reveal that he was an original theologian interested in philosophy. He was also a contemplative, that is, a teacher of the spiritual life, so he had a lifelong interest in what it is to be human. We will return to him again and again in this book.

Theologically, Gregory agrees with his older brother Basil but goes beyond what he had taught. Basil makes a distinction between the divine image and the divine likeness and says our freedom makes it possible to acquire the likeness of God. In creating us, Basil says, God gives us the image, so we are born with it. The likeness is something greater than the image, and God gives us the responsibility of acquiring it. As Basil explains:

"Let us make the human being according to our image and according to our likeness" [Gen. 1:26]. By our creation we have the first, and by our free choice we build the second. In our initial structure co-originates and exists our coming into being according to the image of God. By free choice we are conformed to that which is according to the likeness of God. . . . Now he has made us with the power to become like God. And in giving us the power to become like God, he let us be artisans of the likeness of God, so that the reward for the work would be ours. . . . For I have that which is according to the image in being a rational being, but I become according to the likeness in becoming Christian.[4]

When Basil speaks of "becoming Christian," he means truly living a Christian lifestyle, avoiding sin, practicing spiritual disciplines and all the virtues, and becoming like Christ, that is, like God. Basil says that human freedom can become the artisan, the fashioner, of God's likeness. In his love, God gives us this extraordinary power—to make ourselves like God—in order to give us credit for doing so and reward us for it. Basil compares this process of self-fashioning to the work of a painter. If the artist paints a beautiful canvas, the work receives the attention and admiration; but if an artist adorns himself with beauty, he is the one who is admired.

In this text, Basil does not say freedom is God's likeness, although it makes the likeness possible. He does, however, identify the divine image with reason. As we have seen, in Greek thought reason and freedom go together; without freedom, reason cannot do what it sees is right, and without reason, freedom acts blindly, impulsively, and erratically. So if reason is in God's image, freedom must be in God's image too, as Gregory emphasizes. Gregory says a great deal about the role of freedom in human existence.[5]

Gregory states that God, who is good and indeed transcends all good, created the human being in order to manifest his good-

4. *On the Origin of Humanity* 1.16; trans. Harrison, *St. Basil*, 43–44.
5. Unlike Basil, Gregory of Nyssa does not make a distinction between the image and likeness in Gen. 1:26. In the end, this difference is largely a matter of vocabulary, not the substance of his thought.

ness. God would not give humankind certain parts of his goodness while jealously withholding others; that would not be in line with God's character. So God has given humans the fullness of divine excellence. This gift includes all the virtues, which are, in the first place, divine attributes, such as wisdom, compassion, and love. And this divine excellence is what constitutes the image of God in the human person. It follows, then, that since freedom is included in God's excellence, humans are free too. Following the Greek philosophical tradition, Gregory adds that if humans were not free, neither could they practice any of the virtues, all of which are included in the divine image.[6]

Gregory even says that human "self-determination is equal to God."[7] He means that like the freedom of God, human freedom is self-initiated; its actions are not determined by any external force, not even by God's will. For example, if I choose to smell a rose, it is because I have decided to do so. I have not been made to do it against my will by some force outside myself. In fact, Gregory says that people are able to give birth to themselves, to create themselves as the kind of people they choose to become:

> What is subject to change is in a sense always coming to birth. In mutable nature nothing can be observed which is always the same. Being born, in the sense of constantly experiencing change, does not come about as a result of external initiative, as is the case with the birth of the body. . . . Such a birth occurs by free choice in accordance with whatever form we wish to have, . . . molding ourselves to the principle of either virtue or vice.[8]

For example, a medical student chooses, step by step, to become a doctor. He or she not only studies the physiology of the human body and learns medical skills but also learns a doctor's character, demeanor, and professional ethics. Through many

---

6. *On the Creation of Humanity* 16.10–11; trans. Moore and Wilson, *Gregory*, 405, alt.
7. *On Those Who Have Fallen Asleep*; GNO 9:54.
8. *Life of Moses* 2.3; trans. Malherbe and Ferguson, *Gregory of Nyssa*, 55.

choices over time, the mature medical practitioner comes to birth and grows within that person.

Interestingly, the reason our freedom has such power, according to Gregory, is that we are extremely malleable as human beings. We continually undergo change; we are constantly moving, so we can choose which direction we take. God, however, always remains the same, so clearly not everything about us is like God. Yet our changeableness allows us to choose to become more and more like the divine. The possibilities are wide open, though ultimately, Gregory says, we have two alternatives: virtue or vice, good or evil, the image of God or the image of the devil. We make a lot of complicated decisions in life, and sometimes the moral issues are unclear to us, but in the end our choices make us the kind of people who would be at home in God's Kingdom or in the outer darkness.

God creates everything out of nothing, and Gregory does not believe that human freedom can do that. He says that when we fashion ourselves, we are not absolute creators but are like artisans working with preexisting materials. He compares the human person to a jar that can hold a variety of things. We choose among things outside us and take them into ourselves, using them to fashion what we will become. When we choose wisely, we receive God into ourselves. Since God is infinite and we are finite, we can only receive a limited amount of divine life. The life we receive fills us to capacity and at the same time increases the size of the jar. So we can reach out to God and receive still more, again and again. Thus, when we unceasingly long for God, we are always satisfied yet always strive for more. In this process, our freedom cooperates continually with God's grace.[9] Gregory cites Paul's description of what happens: "Forgetting what lies behind and straining forward to what lies ahead, I press on toward the goal for the prize of the upward call of God in Christ Jesus" (Phil. 3:13–14).[10] Thus we can un-

9. Gregory describes the jar's unending expansion in *On the Soul and the Resurrection*; trans. Roth, *Gregory of Nyssa*, 87–88.
10. See *Life of Moses* 2.225, 242; trans. Malherbe and Ferguson, *Gregory of Nyssa*, 113, 117.

endingly receive more and more divine life. In other words, we are called to eternal growth in God. In the twentieth century, Gregory has become famous for his concept of eternal growth. It is his answer to the question of what our freedom is for. We remain free, however, to choose the other alternative, to try to fill the jar of ourselves with things that are not God, with things that lack ultimate value, with things that leave our longings unsatisfied. Gregory compares this kind of effort to pouring water into a leaky jar.[11] Whatever we pour in leaks out the hole at the bottom, and though we work hard, we remain empty. Gregory says we are also like the Hebrew slaves toiling in Egypt to make bricks. They filled the brick mold with clay, then took the clay out, then refilled it and emptied it, again and again, working endlessly without pay.[12] Gregory's point is that the human person is like a jar created to receive and hold God. We function well when we use our jars for this purpose, but when we try to use them for other purposes, we find they are broken and lead us only to frustration.

The Struggle for Inner Freedom

Gregory of Nyssa's example of the jar shows that when we choose to collaborate with God, our freedom becomes greater, but when we turn away from God, our freedom is far less effective, though we never lose it entirely. Early Christians had learned from Genesis 3 that humankind has chosen to turn away from God and misuse freedom. So Gregory acknowledges that because we are fallen creatures, we do not ordinarily experience the godlike potential of our freedom that he describes. The questions remain: How free are we in daily life? And how can we become more free? How can we come to collaborate in the work of God?

We have to struggle with our freedom, to discover how we can still use it in spite of the constraints of obsessive

11. *On the Beatitudes* 4.6; trans. Hall, "Gregory of Nyssa," 53–55.
12. *Life of Moses* 2.60–62; trans. Malherbe and Ferguson, *Gregory of Nyssa*, 68.

thoughts, unruly emotions, and bad habits. When we first start going to the gym, we may find it hard to do anything because our muscles are weak. But by using them little by little, we can in time grow strong and have much greater freedom of movement. In the same way, with God's help we can train our freedom.

In the fourth, fifth, and sixth centuries, the fathers and mothers of the Egyptian desert were monks and nuns who learned practical wisdom about Christian life from their experience of attempting seriously to live it. The younger ones wrote down the wisdom sayings and stories they learned from their elders, who were good coaches and trainers. Their sayings and stories will help us throughout this book to make concrete and practical for today the early Christian ideas of what it is to be human. The people of the desert can show us how to find the small ways in which we remain free so that by following these ways we can grow in freedom, just as a newcomer to the gym can start with small exercises and in time learn to do more strenuous ones.

Although Gregory of Nyssa presents human choice as facing two alternatives—good and evil—in practice it is much more complicated. There may be two choices at the end—heaven and hell—but along the way there are a wide variety of options. As we seek good, we are free to choose from many good ways to spend our lives, and we can focus on the one that appeals to us, the place where we have a particular talent. Abba Poemen[13] was a wise and compassionate abbot in ancient Egypt and the leader of a large monastic community. Many of his sayings are preserved among the words of the desert fathers. He uses examples to explain the point about different talents and inclinations: "Suppose there are three men living together. One lives a good life in silence, the second is ill but gives thanks to God, the third serves the needs of others with

13. In the Egyptian desert, the monks called older monks who had grown wise through experience "Abba," which means "Father." It is a term expressing affection and respect, and our word "abbot" is derived from it. Wise, older nuns were called "Amma," which means "Mother."

sincerity. These three men are alike, it is as if they were all doing the same work."[14] In the Egyptian desert, where early Christian monasticism was born, men and women experimented with various ways of life as they strove to come close to God. The desert sayings that have come down to us preserve many voices that show what they learned from their experiments. They talked to each other about which way of life is best, that is, which way is most pleasing to God and most effective in bringing a person to the ultimate goal of salvation.

In the words quoted above, Poemen says there are many ways that lead to the goal. He gives the example of three monks living together in a community, and each one is different. One lives a life of silent prayer. He remains alone in order to pray and may not actively serve his neighbors at all, though he loves them and prays for them. The second does not really have a choice of how to live because he is ill. In the ancient desert there was no anesthesia, so he was probably in pain. He has made it his task to give thanks to God even in this situation, a difficult thing to do. The third monk serves other people, but he too works on his inner thoughts and attitudes; he is sincere in his desire to help, not resentful or begrudging. Poemen tells us that all of them are alike. Each spends his lifetime pursuing virtue—that is, excellence of character—in a disciplined way, both inwardly in the heart and outwardly in action.

Another desert story makes a similar point. As often happened, a young monk asks an older one for guidance about how best to live. The older monk responds by passing on wisdom that has been passed down to him from the most reliable sources. He recounts what he has learned from another wise old man, who in turn learned it from a friend of Anthony the Great, the first and most renowned monk of the Egyptian desert:

A brother asked a hermit, "Tell me something good that I may do it and live by it." The hermit said, "God alone knows what

14. Translated in Ward, *Desert Fathers*, 101, alt.

is good. But I have heard that one of the hermits asked the great
Nesteros, who was a friend of Anthony, 'What good work shall
I do?' and he replied, 'Surely all works please God equally?
Scripture says, Abraham was hospitable and God was with him;
Elijah loved quiet and God was with him; David was humble
and God was with him.' So whatever you find you are drawn to
in following God's will, do it and let your heart be at peace."[15]

The brother may have been anxious, thinking he might make
a mistake, miss the target of God's will, and then God would
abandon him. The hermit, like Poemen, reassures him that there
are many good paths and that God is with those who follow each
of them. Thus there are many virtues, so human freedom has
a lot of space in which to move. In fact, he says, this multiplicity is already present in the Bible. The Old Testament heroes
Abraham, Elijah, and David each had a different way of life,
and each pursued a different virtue: hospitality, quiet prayer, and
humility. Each one found God in the life he had chosen. Early
Christians, especially monks, sought to follow the examples of
biblical heroes. So the brother in our story had many examples
to choose from.

Yet the desert Christians found that while there are lots
of good options to choose from, people in this fallen world
have trouble choosing what is good and following through by
putting their good choices into practice. Choices begin in the
mind, where persistent tempting thoughts, unruly emotions,
and bad habits become obstacles that can easily turn us away
from our good intentions. So the Egyptian monks devoted a
great deal of effort to understanding and struggling with their
tempting thoughts. A young monk had a question about this
struggle:

A brother came to Abba Poemen and said to him, "Abba, I have
many thoughts and they put me in danger." The old man led
him outside and said to him, "Expand your chest but do not
breathe in." He said, "I cannot do that." The old man said to

15. Translated in Ward, *Desert Fathers*, 5, alt.

him, "If you cannot do that, no more can you prevent thoughts from arising, but you can resist them."[16]

The young man was new to monastic struggle and was probably overwhelmed by observing all the thoughts in his mind, a discipline that was new to him. Whenever we are awake, thoughts continually arise in our minds. The brother found that his thoughts pulled him in different directions, often away from God. Poemen reassured him that this happens to everybody, just as all people breathe and draw air into their lungs. He need not fear that he will lose his salvation because he cannot stop thoughts from coming, because no one can do that. But he can choose to resist distracting or sinful thoughts and follow good ones.

This kind of mental choice is where human freedom begins its work, for good or ill. "A hermit" in the Egyptian desert "said, 'We are not condemned if bad thoughts enter our minds, but only if we use them badly. Because of our thoughts we may suffer shipwreck, but because of our thoughts we may also earn a crown,'"[17] that is, a reward from God. Another experienced hermit was asked if evil thoughts defile a person. He replied that when a monk immediately pushes away a sinful thought he is undefiled, and when a less-disciplined monk is moved by the thought but struggles and does not act on it, he too is undefiled.[18] So, for example, if one person thinks of stealing a library book and immediately pushes the thought aside while another has the same thought, fantasizes about taking the book home and owning it, but then with greater effort also pushes that thought aside, the book is still in the library. Neither one is a thief, and neither actually made a decision to steal. As Abba Poemen said, a thought is like an axe; if nobody uses it to cut anything, it has no effect.[19]

So what can we do to put sinful thoughts aside? Poemen suggests ignoring them, that is, refusing to engage with them.

16. Poemen 28; trans. Ward, *Sayings*, 171, alt.
17. Translated in Ward, *Desert Fathers*, 110.
18. See Ward, *Desert Fathers*, 108–9.
19. Poemen 15; trans. Ward, *Sayings*, 169.

He says that in time they disintegrate like clothes that are shut carelessly in a chest until they rot, or they are destroyed like a snake or a scorpion that is shut in a bottle and kept there indefinitely.[20] Yet ignoring them may not be enough; when we try to shut them out, they may come back with a vengeance. For a dieter, the thought of eating chocolate may come back every day and occupy the mind more and more insistently. The desert Christians were well aware that more is needed to win the battle with evil thoughts than simply putting them out of one's mind, although that can be a start. Poemen offered another suggestion to a monk engaged in this struggle:

A brother asked Abba Poemen about the harm which he was suffering through his thoughts. The old man said to him, "In this matter it is like a man who has fire on his left and a cup of water on his right. If the fire kindles, he must take water from the cup and extinguish it. The fire is the enemy's seed, and the water is the act of throwing oneself before God."[21]

The desert monks believed that evil thoughts often come from the devil, the enemy of Christians. In this text, the brother is encouraged to pray fervently to God for help every time he is afflicted with sinful thoughts. God is gracious and is able to either make those thoughts disappear or transform them creatively into a source of new insight or into a motivation for good deeds. A woman angry at aggressive panhandlers on the street may pray for them and then realize how hard it is to be homeless and how vulnerable such people are. She may then be moved to donate her money to a homeless shelter instead of giving it to the panhandlers, who might use it for drugs. The important point is that the monk is not expected to overcome evil thoughts by his own strength or willpower. Yet he still has a choice: he can ask God for help.

The desert fathers and mothers were also aware of the large role that habit plays in this struggle for inner transformation.

20. Poemen 20–21; trans. Ward, *Sayings*, 169–70.
21. Poemen 146; trans. Ward, *Sayings*, 187.

When sinful thoughts are part of a long-standing pattern in one's life, it becomes much more difficult to change them. For example, if the master referred to at the beginning of this chapter has been seeing prostitutes for a long time, his habit would make it very difficult for him to turn his mind away from sexual fantasies and desires. A trained and disciplined monk who was encountering a similar temptation for the first time would find it much easier to turn his mind to other things. So even when we are trapped in bad habits, we are still free to do something about them provided we know how to approach the problem. We need to work at it gradually by beginning to change our habits one step at a time. We are free to take a tiny step, and doing so brings us the freedom to take another tiny step, then another, so that slowly we become more free. Even the master could decide not to see a prostitute today and instead pursue a hobby he loves, such as reading and writing poetry. The next day he could make the same decision, and it would be a little easier. When renewed temptations arise, he could find people to encourage him in the change he is making. So, one day at a time, he could persevere in the change he has started. In a similar way, we can eventually break a bad pattern or acquire a new skill with God's help.

Consider the ability to turn the other cheek and to resist returning evil for evil. Christ requires such conduct of his disciples, but in practice it is often very difficult to do. The desert fathers and mothers took this commandment seriously and worked on learning to fulfill it. It is the subject of a conversation between Anthony the Great and fellow monks:

> The brethren came to the Abba Anthony and said to him, "Speak a word; how are we to be saved?" The old man said to them, "You have heard the Scriptures. That should teach you how." But they said, "We want to hear from you too, Father." Then the old man said to them, "The Gospel says, 'If anyone strikes you on one cheek, turn to him the other also'" [Matt. 5:39]. They said, "We cannot do that." The old man said, "If you cannot offer the other cheek, at least allow one cheek to be struck." "We cannot do that either," they said. So he said, "If you are not able to do

that, do not return evil for evil," and they said, "We cannot do that either." Then the old man said to his disciple, "Prepare a little brew of corn for these invalids. If you cannot do this, or that, what can I do for you? What you need is prayers."[22]

Anthony has broken down the task of learning to turn the other cheek into a series of smaller steps, since the brothers cannot do it all at once. If they could learn not to return evil for evil, or even if they found a way to do part of that or struggle toward it, that would be a beginning. Once they learned that, they could work on allowing one cheek to be struck and finally offer the other. It would be like climbing a ladder, one rung at a time. Since they say they cannot do any of what Anthony suggests, they need help from God. As Anthony says, they need prayers.

Another brother was working on the same issue, but he pursued it farther than Anthony's brothers. This monk asked Poemen about not returning evil for evil. What would it mean in practice? What would he have to do to accomplish it? The abbot explains, again breaking the task down into a series of steps, so it can be learned a little at a time.

Another brother questioned [Abba Poemen] in these words: "What does 'See that none of you repays evil for evil' [1 Thess. 5:15 RSV] mean?" The old man said to him, "Passions work in four stages—first, in the heart; secondly, in the face; thirdly, in words; and fourthly, it is essential not to render evil for evil in deeds. If you can purify your heart, passion will not come into your expression; but if it comes into your face, take care not to speak; but if you do speak, cut the conversation short in case you render evil for evil."[23]

In the language of the desert fathers and mothers, "passions" are unruly emotions, in this case probably anger, bitterness, or resentment. In explaining that one learns to follow Christ's difficult commandment step by step, Anthony and Poemen provide

22. Anthony 19; trans. Ward, *Sayings*, 5.
23. Poemen 34; trans. Ward, *Sayings*, 172.

a good example of how to use the freedom we have, though it may seem very small at first, to break down bad habits and build good ones. One can break down the bad habit of obsessive resentful thoughts and build the good habit of treating the difficult neighbor graciously. Clearly we need God's help throughout this struggle. We need God's help to find the kind of goodness best for us to pursue, to put aside evil thoughts, to plead with God for help against temptations, to overcome bad habits, and to cultivate good habits. Prayer was always the heart of the desert life. The monks and nuns prayed in many ways to be receptive to God's word and to cultivate closeness with God, but they also begged for help in their struggles and gave thanks for their good deeds. The work of monks is prayer, and it can and must be chosen. While other people can pray for us, and their prayers certainly help, the desert Christians insisted that each person must pray too. Otherwise, even the prayers of Anthony are not enough. Once a brother who relied on this great monk's prayers but was too lazy to pray himself said to Anthony, "Pray for me." The compassionate old man perceived his attitude and responded with hard words: "I will have no mercy upon you, nor will God have any, if you yourself do not make an effort and if you do not pray to God."[24]

Part of desert prayer was opening oneself to hear God's word in Scripture. How is this accomplished? Again, Poemen explains, it is a question of freely chosen action repeated over time. Hearing comes through listening over and over: "The nature of water is soft, that of stone is hard; but if a bottle is hung above the stone, allowing the water to fall drop by drop, it wears away the stone. So it is with the word of God; it is soft and our heart is hard, but the [person] who hears the word of God often, opens his heart to the fear of God."[25] By fear, Poemen does not mean terror; he surely means reverence, attentiveness, and willingness to do God's will.

24. Anthony 16; trans. Ward, *Sayings*, 4.
25. Poemen 183; trans. Ward, *Sayings*, 192–93.

The message of the desert fathers and mothers is that though
we are sinners, and though the world may tell us we are worthless, it is possible for us to learn, little by little, to become good
people and to do good for others and thus to make a real contribution to society. In the church community, wise and experienced people can coach us, and with practice we can learn.
So ultimately we *can* choose to be transformed for the better,
though it takes work and persistence. In my opinion, this is an
essential part of the good news of Jesus Christ.

Grace and Human Freedom

In the Eastern churches, both in ancient times and today, grace
and human freedom go together. Grace does not conflict with
our capacity to choose but brings our freedom to fullness of
life, creativity, and activity. God, who loves us, wants to work
with us and allows us to share in his work. Origen explains this
collaboration through the example of a sailing ship.

> To what extent should we say that the [sea captain's] skill helps
> in bringing the ship back to the harbor, when compared with
> the force of the winds and the favorable state of the atmosphere
> and the shining of the stars, all of which cooperate to preserve
> those who sail? Why, even the sailors themselves from feelings
> of reverence do not often venture to claim that they have saved
> the ship but attribute it all to God; not that they have performed
> nothing, but that the efforts of God's providence are very much
> greater than the effects of their skill.[26]

The wind filled the sails and enabled the ship to move, the
good weather preserved it from dangerous storms, and the positions of the stars guided the navigator in bringing the ship to
harbor. The sailors were thankful to God for the collaboration
of wind, weather, and stars on their journey. They were well
aware that they could not control the weather or the natural

26. *On First Principles* 3.1.19; trans. Butterworth, *Origen*, 199, alt.

world on which they depended, yet their own work was also necessary to their safe arrival at their destination. Though the contribution of their free choice and work was small in comparison to the natural forces, it was essential. Ancient sailors and desert monks modestly ascribed all their achievements to God, but their work resulted from a happy synergy between God's grace and their own freely chosen actions.

2

God and Christ

As a child I went to a school with a lot of bright kids. Once, when I was twelve years old, we had a class discussion about our identity as human persons. Everybody had a lot to say, and it was taken up again in several of our classes. The last time we discussed the issue, a man from a radio show came and recorded all of us talking vigorously about it in class. It all started with a question: what determines who we are and what we do, heredity or environment, our genes or our upbringing? I could not get a word in edgewise, but I listened. I was thinking surely there must be something else that makes each of us who we are, but nobody raised that question. Finally, as a small group of students were discussing the question during recess, I said, "Surely there must be something else besides heredity and environment." Everybody laughed at me, so I did not mention it again. But I never forgot the question.

Later, in college and after I had become a Christian, I realized that God is the one who makes us who we are. He makes each individual unique so that we are not all photocopies of one another. Each of us reveals God's creativity in a different way. We will discuss human diversity and uniqueness in chapter 9.

And yet, insofar as we are human beings, there are many things we all share, since God has created us in his own image.

The Model and the Image

Early Christians read the Bible in Greek, and when Genesis 1:26 spoke of humankind being made in the image and likeness of God, they connected this verse with Greek philosophical ideas. Platonists thought that the visible and tangible things in the world were images of transcendent, invisible models. They believed that the image derived its beauty and structure from its model. Moreover, its very being was directly connected to the model, though image and model seem to belong to different levels of reality altogether. Yet the model was in contact with the image and made it what it was.

Early Christians borrowed these Platonic concepts and adapted them to their own faith. They believed that because we as human beings are made in God's image, God himself has been our model from the time we were first created. This is a great gift and a great privilege. It means that God has given us something of his beauty and excellence. He is the direct source of our authentic human identity, since the image of God is what defines us as distinctively human. Greek philosophers thought the aim of human existence was to follow God, or become like God, and Christians agreed, though they understood these goals in their own way. It was possible to imagine such a lofty goal because, if we are God's image, the very core of our being is directly connected to him, and he always remains connected with us, creatively renewing his own image in us.

The divine image thus establishes us in a relationship with God. This relationship defines the core of who we are and is the foundation of everything else the divine image and likeness in the human person can become. Gregory of Nyssa reflects on how this happens in a homily on Matthew 5:8, "Blessed are the pure in heart, for they will see God" (NRSV). He begins by asking himself how it could be possible to see God since there is no one who will see God and live (see Exod. 33:20). Because Gregory emphasizes the absolute mystery of God, he wonders what we can hope to see. First, he says that everyone, even non-Christians, can see God's handiwork in the created world and thus know something of the Creator. But then if people are pure in heart, he asks, what more can they see? In answer, he explains the connection between perceiving God and having God within oneself. He begins by comparing it to the difference between knowing about health and actually being healthy:

> The Lord does not say that knowing something about God is blessed, but to possess God in oneself. "Blessed are the pure in heart, for they will see God." He does not seem to me to be offering God as an instant vision to the one whose spiritual eye is purified. But what the grandeur of the text proposes to us is that which the Word [i.e., Jesus] sets out more directly also to others, when he says that the kingdom of God is within us [Luke 17:21]. From this saying we may learn that the person who has purified his own heart from every tendency to passion [that is, unruly emotion] perceives in his own beauty the effulgence of the divine nature.[1]

Gregory then explains that we can find God within ourselves because from the beginning we have been created in the divine image. God is the model and we are, at least originally, the copy. This is why humans are able to perceive God by looking within themselves and there finding his image: "The measure of what is accessible to you is in you, for thus your Maker from the start endowed your essential nature with such good. God has imprinted upon your structure replicas of the good things in his own nature, as though stamping wax with the shape of a design."[2]

In ancient times, people signed documents by putting hot wax on the paper and pressing into the wax a seal carved with their unique design. The wax then bore the seal's imprint and

1. *On the Beatitudes* 6.4; trans. Hall, "Gregory of Nyssa," 69–70, alt.
2. *On the Beatitudes* 6.4; trans. Hall, "Gregory of Nyssa," 70, alt.

showed that the document was theirs. Gregory uses this example to illustrate the meaning of the divine image. God is like the seal, and our human nature is like the wax that shows forth the same design as God, but on a smaller scale.

Notice that the wax receives the imprint by direct contact with the seal, and the copy receives its likeness to the model by direct contact with it. So God is present within his image, making it to be an image of Godself. This point becomes clear later in the same paragraph when Gregory moves on to the example of the sun and a mirror, as we shall see. The very same light that shines from the sun also hits the mirror, is present in its radiant surface, and shines forth from it.

Why, then, do we not easily see God's beauty and goodness in ourselves and in everyone we meet? Gregory compares the image to a mirror and explains that it is covered with dirt. God's light shines onto the mirror, and then the same light is reflected by it. But this does not happen when the mirror is dirty: "Evil, however, overlaying the Godlike pattern, has made the good useless to you, hidden under curtains of shame. If, by conscientious living, you wash away once more the filth that has accumulated on your heart, the Godlike beauty will again shine forth for you."[3] Gregory uses *heart* in the biblical sense, not as the center of sentimentality but as the inner human being. He then employs the image of polished iron, which can function as a mirror when not covered with rust.

> When iron is stripped of rust by a whetstone, what once was dull itself shines as it faces the sun and gives forth beams and shafts of light. So also, when the inner human being, which is what the Lord calls "the heart," has wiped off the rusty filth that has spread by evil decay over its form, it will again recover its likeness to its model and be good. What is like the good [i.e., God] is surely good.[4]

That is, once we are restored from our fallen condition to holiness through repentance, we can see God's likeness within

3. *On the Beatitudes* 6.4; trans. Hall, "Gregory of Nyssa," 70, alt.
4. *On the Beatitudes* 6.4; trans. Hall, "Gregory of Nyssa," 70, alt.

ourselves. One cannot stare at the sun but can see its rays in a mirror. This is how the pure in heart see God, whom the saints cannot see and live. "Therefore," Gregory concludes, "the one who looks at himself sees in himself what he desires, and so the pure in heart becomes blessed, because by looking at his own purity he perceives the model in the copy."[5] And part of what this person sees is that the purity within his or her heart is God's own purity and has come to him or her as a gift.

Gregory shows how the image of God in which we are made is what enables us to be in relationship with God and grow in that relationship. The divine image makes possible participation in the life and goodness of God. Moreover, this participation enables the vision of God because, as Plato and with him many in the ancient world believed, "like is known by like."[6]

According to early Christian writers, from the beginning God created humankind in God's own image, thus establishing a relationship with human beings as a defining characteristic of who they are. Yet humans fell, breaking that relationship. The fall did not eradicate the divine image but instead, in Gregory of Nyssa's metaphors, covered it with dirt or rust. So God sent his Son Christ, who became human in order to restore the divine image in all of humanity. The rest of this chapter will discuss early Christian ideas of how we were created in the image of God and of Christ, how we fell away from our task of becoming like God, and how God restores us in Jesus Christ.

Creation in the Image of God

God's creation of human beings is an expression of his love. Clement of Alexandria, a second-century Christian theologian, depicts this love in an extraordinary way. He combines the first creation story, about God's image (Gen. 1), with the second creation story, in which God fashions the human being from the earth and breathes into him the breath of life (Gen. 2).

5. *On the Beatitudes* 6.4; trans. Hall, "Gregory of Nyssa," 70, alt.
6. For more on this, see pp. 31–32.

The human being, then, is naturally a friend of God, since indeed he is his creation. And other things have been made by a command alone, while God fashioned the human being with his own hands and breathed in something of his own [breath] [see Gen. 2:7]. Now, one whom God has fashioned and made in his own image [see Gen. 1:26] is either created as desirable to God himself, or fashioned as desirable for the sake of another. If, then, the human being is desirable in himself, God, who is good, has loved what is good, and the love-charm is within the human being—that which indeed is called a breath of God.[7]

We were created to be friends of God, so it is natural for us to be his friends. So when we sin in ways that sever that friendship, we are going against our own nature as humans. Today people think of human nature as fundamentally flawed or sinful—"It's only human nature," they say. Early Greek-speaking Christians thought of our nature, what we fundamentally *are*, as good and considered sin to be a distortion of that nature. This point has big implications. It means that we do not have to choose between God and our own integrity. When we come close to God, we become whole as human beings; in other words, we become authentically who we are.

In the text quoted above, Clement says that God expressed his love for us first by holding us in his own hands as he made us and then by breathing into us something of his own, namely, his breath. He created other things differently, just by a word: "Let there be . . ." The sharing of breath connects God with the human person. This, in turn, signifies other kinds of connections too, connections between God's goodness and human goodness and between God as model and the human as image. Thus, Clement says, out of love God created us and placed within us something of his own that would make him desire us; he breathed his breath into us, which also signifies the divine image, and this becomes a love-charm for him. So God is drawn to love us, yet no one but himself constrains God to love. He created us as the kind of persons he would love.

7. *Paedagogus* 1.3; ed. Marrou, *Clément d'Alexandrie*, 122.

Creation in the image of God also establishes a relationship between Christ and humankind. Early Christians made a distinction between the Image, that is, Christ, who is entirely like the Father, and humans, who are made "*in* the image," as it says in Genesis 1:27. In this book I have continued the modern practice of calling human beings "the image and likeness of God," instead of saying "*in* the image" each time. But I would ask readers to remember the difference between Christ, who is perfectly like God the Father, and human beings, whose likeness to God can never be complete.

This distinction means that from the time of our creation, long before he became incarnate, Christ, God's true and faithful Image, was the model according to whom humans were made "*in* the image." So because we are images of Christ, we are also images of God the Father, though never as completely as Christ is. Clement's successor as a Christian teacher in Alexandria, Origen, explains "the difference between what is 'in the image of God' [Gen. 1:27 RSV] and his Image [see Col. 1:15]" as follows: "The Image of God is . . . the very Logos and truth, and further, the very wisdom himself, being 'the image of his goodness' [Wis. 7:26], whereas the human was made 'in the image of God,' and, furthermore, every human of whom Christ is head is God's image and glory [see 1 Cor. 11:3, 7]."[8] Notice Origen says that that which is in the image in humans is strengthened when they are members of the church. When Christ is their head and they become his body, they have a closer connection with their model, so through Christ's mediation they are "God's image and glory."

Origen, following John 1:1, calls the one who would become incarnate as Jesus Christ the "Logos," usually translated as the "Word." *Logos* actually means a number of things that cannot be captured quickly in English. It means God's word, speech, discourse, and self-expression, as well as God's rationality that creates, structures, and governs the universe in an orderly way. According to Greek philosophy, especially Stoicism, human be-

---

8. *Against Celsus* 6.63; trans. Chadwick, *Origen*, 378, alt.

ings are also endowed with rationality, which links them with the divine and distinguishes them from other animals. Humans are *logikoi*, rational, so they share in the Logos. Following John, Christians adopted this philosophical idea and transformed it to mean that Christ is the Logos and is thus the model for humans, who participate in his character as Logos. So humans are rational (*logikoi*) precisely as his image.

The close verbal and conceptual connection between the divine Word and humans, who are by definition rational animals, is impossible to translate directly into English. But keep it in mind as we consider the fourth-century archbishop Athanasius of Alexandria's description of Christ's role in human creation. Like his predecessor Clement, Athanasius begins with the Creator's goodness:

> For God is good, or rather is the source of goodness; as good, he does not become envious of anybody. So, envying existence to nobody, he has created all things out of nothing by his own Word [*Logos*], our Lord Jesus Christ. And above all those on earth he granted mercy to humankind. Seeing that they were not capable, according to the principle of their own creation, of remaining eternally, he gave them something greater. He did not simply create human beings like all the non-rational animals on earth; but according to his own image he created them, sharing with them also the power of his own Word, that becoming rational [*logikoi*], as possessing a shadow of the Word, they may be able to remain in blessedness, living the true life and being in paradise with the saints.[9]

In ancient times, humans were seen as different from other animals in that humans possessed reason.[10] Athanasius also links this reason to the divine image, which is distinctively human, since humans possess a shadow—a kind of image—of the Word, who is the source of rationality. Yet, Athanasius adds, the Word, who is divine, is also the source of life and immortality. So when

---

9. *On the Incarnation* 4.3; ed. Cross, *Athanasius*, 5
10. On the positive relationship of humans with other animals, a very important facet of the divine image, see chapter 7.

God created humans in his image and thus linked them with himself, he bestowed eternal life on them, which would flow from God to humans as long as they remained linked to their divine Source.

The Fall of Humankind

According to Athanasius, humans could have remained immortal by continuing to look toward the Word and staying connected to him. Then the Word—who is God (John 1:1), the second person of the Trinity, and thus the source of life—would live in them. They needed to keep the divine life within themselves because they were created out of nothingness. As created beings, they began their lives through a change from nothingness to being, so at the root of their existence there is change and a mixture of being with nonbeing. The presence of change and nonbeing within them makes humans inherently unstable, Athanasius believes, susceptible to disintegration into nothingness, that is, death. Yet when God, or the Word, who is eternal life, dwells within them he stabilizes the human being, counteracting their inherent tendency to disintegrate when left to themselves.

The trouble is that humankind did not choose to remain close to God. Athanasius describes the fall as follows:

> For God has not only created us out of nonbeing, but also granted us to live in accordance with God by the grace of the Word. But as human beings turned away from eternal things, and by the devil's counsel turned toward corruptible things, they became for themselves the cause of corruption in death. Being, as I said before, by nature corruptible, by the grace of their participation in the Word they escaped what accords with nature, if they remained good. For through the presence of the Word within them, the corruption according to nature did not come near them, as indeed Wisdom has rightly said: "God created the human being for incorruption and made him an image

of his own eternity; but through the devil's envy death entered the world" [Wis. 2:23–24 RSV, alt.].[11]

People were immortal not by nature but by grace. Eternal life is linked, according to Athanasius, to living in accord with God and thus to goodness, since God is absolute good and the source of goodness as well as the source of life. In the fall, the devil tempted people to sever their link with God and turn away from goodness so that they no longer lived in accord with God. Then they became subject to disintegration, and God's work of creation started to unravel.

According to Athanasius, the fall began with a choice to "turn away from eternal things" to other things of lesser value. As humans we choose where to focus our attention, where to turn our eyes, how to spend our time, and how to arrange our priorities. We make these choices from minute to minute as we pass through each day. It is easy to get distracted from what is best and to become entangled in distracting thoughts, feelings, sounds, and pictures so that imperceptibly we come to put them first in our lives instead of God. Remember how Gregory of Nyssa described the image of God in the human person as a mirror reflecting divine light? He also described the fall as a choice to turn the mirror that is our self away from God, so that we are no longer filled with his light, and toward the things of this world that come and go and disintegrate so that we reflect them and thus become like them.[12]

The Restoration of the Image

According to Athanasius, the fall put God in a dilemma. On the one hand, his creative handiwork was disintegrating, but on the other hand, he did not want to violate the integrity of human beings, whom he had made free and who had used their

11. *On the Incarnation* 5.1–2; ed. Cross, *Athanasius*, 8, alt. For Athanasius, as for Origen, the Wisdom of Solomon was a book of inspired Scripture.
12. *On the Creation of Humanity* 12.9–10; trans. Moore and Wilson, *Gregory*, 398–99.

freedom to choose death. Athanasius sees the incarnation of Christ as God's creative response to this dilemma:

> What, then, did God have to do? Or what had to happen, except that that which is according to the image would again be renewed, so that through it human beings might again be able to know God? And how could this happen except by the coming near of the Image of God himself, our Savior Jesus Christ? For through human beings it was not possible, since indeed they were made *according* to the image; but neither was it possible through the angels, for they are not images [of God]. Therefore the Word of God came near through himself, that as Image of the Father he would be able to recreate the human being according to the image.[13]

Human beings are made according to the image, and only Christ is the Image in an absolute sense; he is the model according to which we were made in the beginning. So once the image in us has been covered with dirt by the fall, only he can restore it. Athanasius compares this restoration to the work of an artist restoring a picture he has made:

> You know what happens when a portrait that has been painted on a panel becomes obliterated through external stains. The artist does not throw away the panel, but the subject of the portrait has to come and sit for it again, and then the likeness is redrawn on the same material. In this way also, the all-holy Son of the Father, being an Image of the Father, came near to our place, that he might renew the human being made in accord with himself. . . . Therefore also he said to the Jews: "Unless one is born anew . . ." [John 3:3 RSV]. He did not mean birth from one's mother, as they suspected, but the rebirth and re-creation of the soul, showing forth that which is according to the image.[14]

Here Athanasius shows Christ fulfilling two functions as he restores the image in humankind. As God, he is the artist re-

---

13. *On the Incarnation* 13.7; ed. Cross, *Athanasius*, 21, emphasis mine.
14. *On the Incarnation* 14.1–2; ed. Cross, *Athanasius*, 21–22. The first two sentences are from the anonymous translation of a religious of CSMV, 41; the rest is my translation.

creating the image in us. As man, he is the model according to which the image in each of us is made, the model who has come to dwell in this world, the Creator's art studio.

From Adam to Christ

Irenaeus, a disciple of the martyred Bishop Polycarp of Smyrna, who was himself a disciple of the apostle John, migrated in the second century from Asia Minor to France, where he became the bishop of Lyons and one of the first great Christian theologians. In other words, he lived in the West but came from the East. He wrote in Greek, and although the originals are lost, his works have come down to us in ancient Latin and Armenian translations. His writings show how all of history and the whole world are included within God's plan of salvation. The later Greek-speaking writers we have been studying built on the foundations he laid. But he can help us see the broader picture of salvation, a picture in which Athanasius's idea of Christ restoring the divine image is a central part.

A key concept in Irenaeus's theology comes from Ephesians 1:9–10: "For [God the Father] has made known to us in all wisdom and insight the mystery of his will, according to his purpose which he set forth in Christ as a plan for the fullness of time, to recapitulate all things in him, things in heaven and things on earth" (alt.). The word *recapitulate* is a literal translation of both the Greek word that Irenaeus used and the Latin translation of it in his writings. For him, recapitulation names God's process of restarting humankind in Christ, renewing and restoring it in the divine image and likeness. The word *recapitulation* literally means "reheading." Christ replaces Adam as the head of humankind, and, to borrow Paul's metaphor, the new head becomes attached to the body. Christ's body is all the members of the church, which follows him instead of the old Adam. This reheading presupposes that people are by nature connected to one another, that humankind is united as a whole. Christ has become the new leader of this whole, so potentially all people can choose to unite themselves with him instead of with Adam, to trust and follow him, and thus become members of his body. By doing so, according to Irenaeus, they will benefit from his saving work. The process of recapitulation has three aspects, and Christ accomplishes all of them at once. First, it is a *repetition* of the creation of humankind—a new beginning—in which Christ is the new Adam. Second, it is a *reversal* of what went wrong in the fall. Adam messed up the first time, but Christ does it right this time and establishes a new pattern, a new kind of existence for people to follow. Third, it is a *summation* of all of human history throughout the world so that all people can be united with Christ in a new humankind. We will examine these aspects of recapitulation in order.

Like Athanasius, Irenaeus believes that because of sin humankind became subject to death and that release from death is central to salvation in Christ. In Adam, the first-formed man with whom we are united at the outset, we all die; but if we unite ourselves to Christ and die in him, we will also rise with him. When he becomes incarnate, the Lord shares our flesh, and for Irenaeus this shared flesh is what unites him with all people and enables the resurrection of his flesh to spread to others. He explains it this way:

> Everyone is implicated in the initial fashioning of Adam, and we were bound to death through the disobedience. So it was appropriate [for us] to be loosed from death through the obedience of the One who on our account became human [see Rom. 5:12, 19]. Death reigned over the flesh, so when it was abolished through flesh, it was necessary that it release the human from its oppression. "The Word became flesh" [John 1:14], so by means of the flesh, which sin had dominated, death would be abolished and no longer be in us. And for this reason the Word received the same embodiment as the one initially fashioned, so that he could fight for the fathers and conquer in Adam that which had struck us in Adam.[15]

15. *Demonstration of the Apostolic Preaching* 31; trans. Behr, *St. Irenaeus*, 60–61, alt. Here and on the next two pages, in consultation with him, I have reworked John Behr's translation from the Armenian of the *Demonstration*.

By taking on human flesh, Christ is united to humankind "in Adam," and from that location he can make a new beginning and become a new head within humankind for others to follow. In this way, he can save Adam and all his human ancestors: Eve, Abraham, Sarah, David, and all the saints of the Hebrew Bible.

Notice how this passage includes the second aspect of recapitulation, namely, reversal of what went wrong in the fall. Irenaeus says that death conquered human flesh, but Christ's flesh conquers death. Similarly, he says elsewhere that as the virgin Eve disobeyed God and brought death, the virgin Mary obeyed God and gave birth to life. Further, as Adam fell through a tree in paradise, Christ saves us through the tree of the cross. Christ's reversals of fallen patterns can save us because he became man according to the image and likeness of God (Gen. 1:26–27) and restored that image and likeness by re-creating the original patterns of human cooperation with God.[16]

A little later, Irenaeus more clearly explains the process of recapitulation:

> God the Father was rich in mercy. He sent the creative Word, who, as he came to save us, was in the same place and situation where we were when we lost life. He broke the bonds of the prison. His light appeared and dispelled the prison's darkness. His light sanctified our birth and abolished death, loosening the same bonds that had trapped us. And he demonstrated the resurrection, becoming himself "the first-born from the dead" [Col. 1:18 RSV]. He raised in himself the fallen human, raising him above to the highest heaven, to the right hand of the Father's glory, as God had promised.[17]

Notice that Irenaeus says Christ sanctified our birth. He went through human birth himself, and now that humankind can hope for eternal life instead of futility and disintegration, the

---

16. *Demonstration of the Apostolic Preaching* 32–33; trans. Behr, *St. Irenaeus*, 61.
17. *Demonstration of the Apostolic Preaching* 37; trans. Behr, *St. Irenaeus*, 64, alt.

beginning of every new human life has become a source of joy for those who look toward the end that God has planned. This text also reveals the goal in the age to come, the purpose of human history toward which Irenaeus looks. Indeed, he sees divine providence as guiding all of our past and future toward this goal. In recapitulation, Christ sums up humankind across all time and space, provided they are willing, by uniting all to himself. This is the third aspect of recapitulation. Irenaeus shows how this happens first in the history recounted in Hebrew Scripture:

> The prophets were sent here from God. By the Holy Spirit they admonished the people and returned them to the God of the patriarchs, the Almighty. They were made heralds of the revelation of our Lord Jesus Christ, the Son of God. They announced that his flesh would blossom from the seed of David [see Isa. 11:1]. So, according to the flesh, he would be son of David, who was the son of Abraham through a long succession [see Matt. 1:1]. Yet, according to the Spirit, he would be Son of God. At first he was with the Father, born before all creation. And at the close of the age he was revealed to all the world as human, "recapitulating all things" in himself, the Word of God, "things in heaven and things on earth" [Eph. 1:10 RSV, alt.].[18]

Thus while the patriarchs and kings are literally Christ's ancestors, who prepared a place for him in Israel, the prophets announced beforehand what Christ would accomplish. Irenaeus believes that Christ's salvation will continue to be worked out in history, particularly the history of the church, until the final consummation. The passage above ends by saying that since he is both God and man, Christ unites in himself heaven and earth, the two levels of the cosmos, as it was known in antiquity. A bit later, Irenaeus uses a traditional symbol of the cross reaching to the four points of the compass—north and south, east and west—to show that Christ unites the entire earth with himself and brings it

---

18. *Demonstration of the Apostolic Preaching* 30; trans. Behr, *St. Irenaeus*, 60, alt.

all to the Father.[19] Thus Irenaeus shows that each human person, made in God's image, is saved as part of the whole cosmos and as a member of a human community. We will discuss these themes of cosmos and community further in chapters 7 and 9.

The Source of Our Human Identity

This chapter has shown that God makes me who I am and that he remains linked to me because I am made in his image. This answers the question I asked as a child about where my identity as a human being comes from. Underlying that question was the thought that in order for me to have significance and value, I cannot be only the product of my genes or my environment. This question is prompted by the dehumanizing world in which we live. "If I do not have real value," I asked myself, "how can I produce real value in myself, or how can I do anything of genuine value? I cannot make something out of nothing." The good news is that God, who has created the world out of nothing, has made all human persons—everyone, without exception—to be people of real value, for he has placed his own value, the divine image, in each of us.

In the ancient Roman army, soldiers wore large, magnificent cloaks as part of their uniforms. A certain soldier once wondered whether God could ever forgive his sins, and he asked this of one of the desert fathers, Abba Mius. The soldier was tormented by his anxiety, and underlying it was the question whether he could have any real value. This other question must have been why the answer that God forgives sins seemed so unconvincing to him, like a trivial platitude, even after they had talked about it for a long time. Mius was gentle and patient and finally came up with an answer the soldier could accept. A record of their conversation has come down to us:

> A soldier asked Abba Mius if God accepted repentance. After the old man had taught him many things he said, "Tell me, my

19. *Demonstration of the Apostolic Preaching* 34; trans. Behr, *St. Irenaeus*, 62.

dear, if your cloak is torn, do you throw it away?" He replied, "No, I mend it and use it again." The old man said to him, "If you are so careful about your cloak, will not God be equally careful about his creature?"[20]

God created us according to his image and likeness and restores us when we are fallen. He does this because he loves us.

---

20. Mius 3; trans. Ward, *Sayings*, 150.

3

Spiritual Perception

In ancient Greco-Roman society, actors were despised instead of admired as they are today. They tended to come from the lower classes, and Christians worried about baptizing them because they were thought to have sinful lifestyles. On stage, they wore masks to show which character they were playing, so the same actor could be a king in act 1 and come back in a different mask in act 3 to play a slave. Of course, in real life he was neither a king nor a slave.

John Chrysostom was a great preacher in Antioch in the second half of the fourth century. In fact, people gave him the nickname "Chrysostom," which means "Golden Mouth," because of his preaching. Although he came from a privileged family and had a fine education, he was an advocate for the poor his entire life. In a sermon on the rich man and Lazarus (Luke 16:19–31), he told his congregation about how little meaning wealth and poverty have in determining who we really are as human beings. He used the analogy of a play to explain what he meant:

> For just as on the stage actors enter with the masks of kings, generals, doctors, teachers, professors, and soldiers, without

themselves being anything of the sort, so in the present life
poverty and wealth are only masks. If you are sitting in the
theater and see one of the actors wearing the mask of a king,
you do not call him fortunate or think that he is a king, nor
would you wish to become what he is; but since you know that
he is some tradesman, perhaps a rope-maker or a coppersmith
or something of the sort, you do not call him fortunate because
of his mask and his costume, nor do you judge his social class
by them. . . . In the same way even here, sitting in this world
as if in a theater and looking at the players on the stage, when
you see many rich people, do not think that they are truly rich,
but that they are wearing the masks of rich people. Just as that
man who acts the part of king or general on the stage often
turns out to be a household servant or somebody who sells figs
or grapes in the market, so also the rich man often turns out to
be the poorest of all.[1]

This text speaks volumes about the hierarchy, snobbery, and
class prejudice in Greco-Roman society. But John names his
audience's prejudices in order to keep them with him. Then he
takes them to an entirely different place, where God's judgment
will turn their prejudices upside down. He explains why the rich
man is actually the poorest:

If you take off his mask, open up his conscience, and enter into
his mind, you will often find there a great poverty of virtue: you
will find that he belongs to the lowest class of all. Just as in the
theater, when evening falls and the audience departs, and the
kings and generals go outside to remove the costumes of their
roles, they are then revealed to everyone appearing to be exactly
what they are; so also now when death arrives and the theater
is dissolved, everyone takes off the masks of wealth and poverty
and departs to the other world. When all are judged by their
deeds alone, some are shown to be truly wealthy, others poor,
some of high class, others of no account.[2]

1. *Second Sermon on Lazarus and the Rich Man*; trans. Roth, *St. John Chrysostom*, 46–47.
2. *Second Sermon on Lazarus and the Rich Man*; trans. Roth, *St. John Chrysostom*, 47, alt.

Thus John is saying wealth, poverty, and social class are not our real identities as human beings. They are roles we play, and they are temporary. Hidden beneath them is the human person that each of us truly is. This is the person God sees, and it may be very different from the one others who are prejudiced see and judge. John says, further, that our standing in the life to come depends on our virtues, that good character is what we can take with us. Our character determines who we really are now and who we will be in eternity.

Virtues are central to the likeness of God, and we will discuss them in the next chapter. But John Chrysostom's story about the theater raises another issue. It is clear that when we look at those around us, we often do not see them as they really are. We may see reflections of our own prejudices, or we may see the masks they have to wear in order to function in society. How, then, can I know my neighbor as she really is? If I see her truly, surely I will see the image of God, and then I may easily be moved to love her.

Dorotheus of Gaza, a sixth-century desert abbot, asks us to imagine a circle with God in the center and us and our neighbors around the rim. When we and our neighbors move closer to each other, the circle gets smaller so that we also move closer to the center and to God. And when we move closer to God, we also move closer to our neighbors.[3] Thus love for God and love for neighbor naturally go together. As Jesus says, "You shall love the Lord your God with all your heart, and with all your soul, and with all your mind. This is the great and first commandment. And a second is like it, You shall love your neighbor as yourself. On these two commandments depend all the law and the prophets" (Matt. 22:37–40). So before asking how we can perceive our neighbors, we will ask how we can perceive God. If we see something of God, we will be able to recognize his image in our neighbors.

3. Dorotheus of Gaza, *On Refusal to Judge Our Neighbor*; trans. Wheeler, *Dorotheos of Gaza*, 138–39.

The Vision of God

"The glory of God is a human being fully alive," says Irenaeus. Years ago I saw these words on a poster in the theology department hallway at a college somewhere. This message seems to say that whatever activity we think makes us fully alive will bring glory to God. But this understanding is misleading; it is not what Irenaeus says. The second half of his sentence is important: "and the life of a human being is the vision of God."[4] For Irenaeus, to see God is the final goal of human existence. Such vision brings with it participation in the life of God, which is indeed eternal life. Eternal life goes with vision because those who are enabled to see God have been transformed into a state more like God's than our present condition. God has given them a share in his own eternal existence, allowing them to truly see him. Thus the vision itself is entirely God's gift. Irenaeus believes that as Christians we spend our whole lives on earth preparing for this vision, slowly being educated by God so that we will be able to see him when the time comes.

The ability to perceive God and other people spiritually is an important facet of the divine image in us, though our perceptions are clouded because of the fall. We saw in the last chapter that human reason was considered an image of the divine Logos, or Reason, who became incarnate as Jesus Christ. Today *reason* is understood much more narrowly than it was in the ancient world. People now connect reason with logic, mathematics, and scientific inferences from cause to effect or from effect to cause. The word for this kind of reason is *ratio* in Latin and *dianoia* in Greek. People in ancient and medieval times understood and valued this kind of reason, and indeed early Christians saw in it the divine image (we will discuss this type of reason in chapter 8). Yet people in ancient and medieval times also recognized a higher kind of rationality and gave it a different name: *intellectus* in Latin and *nous* in Greek. This kind of "spiritual intellect" is

4. *Against Heresies* 4.20.7; trans. Saward, *Scandal of the Incarnation*, 44, alt.

able to perceive spiritual realities and is closely connected with free choice, wisdom, and virtue.

Today most people probably do not even know they have a *nous* because they are occupied with many outward, visible things and their spiritual perception is blocked by neglect or sin. Yet by God's grace this power of spiritual perception can be rediscovered through the process of education Irenaeus recommends, that is, through the practice of a disciplined life of prayer and service.

Like Irenaeus, Gregory of Nyssa believes that the vision of God is the goal of human existence. In Genesis 2:7, God molds the human body from the earth and breathes into it his own breath. This verse may lie behind Gregory's statement that God mixed together a "divine and intellectual essence" and earthly elements to make the human being, "a likeness of the divine transcendent power." Gregory immediately adds that in saying this he has paraphrased Genesis 1:27, "And God created the human in the image of God" (NRSV, alt.).[5] Gregory does not mean to say that human beings are divine. But something in them does derive from the divine, as breath comes from lungs; something human is connected to the divine and therefore is *like* the divine.

Gregory then explains that the two components from which the human person is made—divine breath and earth—belong to two distinct levels of reality: (1) the invisible world of angels and spiritual realities, which is above the heavens, and (2) the earth we can touch. These are the two levels of reality in which Plato and many other Greek philosophers believe. These two levels are distinguished from each other by the different ways in which humans perceive them. With the bodily senses of sight, hearing, touch, and the like, humans can perceive the material world, which is known as the visible world. This is "the world" as we know it today; it is the reality that scientists examine, test, and measure. Yet according to ancient philosophers and Christians, there is also a world invisible to the bodily senses, the world

5. *On Infants' Early Deaths*; GNO 3.2:77.

of God and the angels, which we can perceive with the *nous*, that is, the mind or "intellect." The mind not only organizes data we obtain through sight and touch but also perceives and receives spiritual realities. It is the part of us that belongs to the spiritual world, a world the *nous* can "see." By awakening our minds through disciplined prayer, we can, with God's grace, become capable of seeing God.

Because we can perceive both the spiritual realm and the physical earth, we belong to both and are connected to both. We live not only with God and the angels but also with the animals and plants. Yet, Gregory asks himself, why did God create humans from a combination of spiritual and material realities? In other words, why were humans made to live on earth with the same kind of intellect that angels in heaven have, the same ability to perceive spiritual realities? Gregory's answer is that in this way angels and humans together will be able to know God and thus glorify God. In glorifying God together, they will become united with each other and can thus unite the heavenly and earthly worlds of which each is a part.[6]

When people glorify God in this way, according to Gregory, they "look upon God." Adoration and vision occur together. Thus those who glorify God will come to see him, and those who see him will glorify him. They receive God's gift of himself as one they can perceive, and in turn they give him their praise.

Gregory adds that looking upon God nourishes the one who looks, for such looking is a source of life to the mind, since the mind is, in some way, like God. Just as food nourishes the body, he says, the vision of God nourishes the mind, or the spiritual side of our human nature. This is because those who see God also receive God's life into themselves.[7] Eating food is a graphic metaphor for this spiritual participation. So, as Irenaeus says, the vision of God truly becomes *life* for the human being.

Gregory presupposes that like is known by like, something many Greek philosophers believed. This belief, shared by many

6. *On Infants' Early Deaths*; trans. Moore and Wilson, *Gregory*, 375.
7. *On Infants' Early Deaths*; trans. Moore and Wilson, *Gregory*, 375–76.

in the ancient world, implies that in order for the human person to know God there must be something within the human itself that is like God. Similarly, it was thought that the eye must contain light in itself so as to be able to see light. So the mind, which perceives the divine, must be the image and likeness of God, as Gregory says. He explains what he means by an analogy between the intellect and the bodily eyes:

> The eye enjoys the light through having natural light within itself to grasp its kindred light. The finger or any other limb cannot produce the act of vision because none of this natural light is incorporated into any of them. The same necessity requires that in our participation in God there should be some kinship in the structure of the one who enjoys with that in which he participates. Therefore, as the scripture says, the human was made in the image of God [see Gen. 1:27]. Like, I take it, may be able to see like. And to see God is . . . the life of the soul.[8]

When we see the beauty of a sunset over the ocean or the detailed petals of a tiger lily in bloom or the golden white and black stripes shimmering on a cat's fur, we are delighted with the things we see. Yet we see something more when we see God in the things he has made. The natural world becomes a window or a door into God's presence. When this happens, we see with a kind of double vision. We see the sunset, the tiger lily, and the cat as they are in themselves, which is delightful, but we also see through to the presence of God, who is within them and beyond them; and this is a further joy. Thus through both our eyes and our spiritual perception we are at one with the natural world and with God.

Wounded Spiritual Eyes and Their Cure

Why, then, is such vision a rare occurrence? Why don't we see God in and through the things around us all the time? Our spiri-

---

8. *On Infants' Early Deaths*; GNO 3.2:79–80; trans. Moore and Wilson, *Gregory*, 375–76, alt.

tual eyes are wounded because we have fallen away from God. This is ultimately why people today do not even know they have a capacity for spiritual perception. We are like people who are born blind but are able to receive sight.

So what has gone wrong? Basil, Gregory's brother, describes the origin of the fall as the turning of an eye, a small movement that can have a devastating effect. He uses this metaphor to show how sin could have originated with one wrong choice, a small turn away from God, the source of light: "With a small turning of the eye, we are either facing the sun or facing the shadow of our own body. Thus one who looks upward easily finds illumination, but for one who turns toward the shadow, darkening is inevitable."[9] Thus evil, Basil concludes, is a result of free choice. Gregory of Nyssa also compares the sinful condition to closing one's eyes to the light or having diseased eyes and neglecting the doctor's orders that would heal them.[10] So in our fallen condition, we find we are unable to perceive God, though we were originally created with the capacity to do so.

Further, Athanasius explains that we became involved in idolatry because we were unable to see the true God:

> Human beings, foolish as they are, thought little of the grace they had received, and turned away from God. They defiled their own soul so completely that they not only lost their apprehension of God, but invented for themselves other gods of various kinds. They fashioned idols for themselves in place of the truth and reverenced things that are not, rather than God who is, as St. Paul says, worshiping "the creature rather than the Creator" [Rom. 1:25 RSV]. . . . Neither God nor his Word was known. Yet he had not hidden himself from the sight of humans, nor given the knowledge of himself in one way only; but rather he had unfolded it in many forms and by many ways.[11]

9. *That God Is Not the Cause of Evil* 8; trans. Harrison, *St. Basil*, 76.
10. *On Virginity* 12; trans. Callahan, *Gregory of Nyssa*, 43. See also *On Infants' Early Deaths*; trans. Moore and Wilson, *Gregory*, 376.
11. *On the Incarnation* 11; trans. Anonymous, *St. Athanasius*, 38–39, alt.

Athanasius then summarizes all the ways God sought to communicate with humankind in the Hebrew Bible, namely, through creation itself and through the law and the prophets. All this, says Athanasius, was "a sacred school of the knowledge of God and the conduct of the spiritual life for the whole world,"[12] not simply for the Jewish people. Yet the message did not get through. Instead, the fallen condition continued to get worse. The mind no longer functioned in such a way as to enable our perception of God. Athanasius calls this lack of function "the dehumanizing of humankind,"[13] since in his view perception of God and communion with him are essential to living authentically human lives.

In addition to outright idolatry, misperception of spiritual realities is a dangerous consequence of the fall. John Cassian was a fifth-century monk who spent his youth in the Egyptian desert but later moved to France, where he was abbot of a religious community. He wrote down stories of the desert fathers and mothers to instruct his French community about monastic life. He tells of some Egyptian monks who lived intense lives of solitary prayer but were misled by spiritual delusion. One was misled into throwing himself into a well with the idea that God would protect him because of his own righteousness. With great effort, the brothers pulled him out, but he died two days later. Another monk conversed regularly but unknowingly with the devil, who had taken on the form of an angel. The devil told him to kill his son, who was living with him, so as to be as holy as Abraham. Fortunately, his son guessed what was happening and ran away. According to Cassian, such disasters can be avoided if monks ask for a second opinion about their visions from other experienced monks before acting on them.[14] In this way, they can benefit from shared wisdom, and they will practice humility instead of assuming that their own experiences or ideas must be right.

12. *On the Incarnation* 12; trans. Anonymous, *St. Athanasius*, 40.
13. *On the Incarnation* 13; trans. Anonymous, *St. Athanasius*, 40, alt.
14. *Conference* 2.5, 7, 10; trans. Luibheid, *John Cassian*, 64–65, 66, 67.

Because fallen human beings could not perceive God and instead were immersed in material things, worshiped idols, or strayed into spiritual delusion, Athanasius sees God as facing an obstacle to his creative work. What was he to do? People had lost authentic awareness of spiritual realities and their attention was focused on earthly things, that is, the things they could see with their eyes and touch with their hands. Again, as with the problem of humans disintegrating in death, God's solution is the incarnation of the Word, who uses the communication skills of a good educator:

> Desiring to do good to humans, as Human he comes, taking to himself a body like the rest; and through his actions done in that body, as it were on their own level, he teaches those who would not learn by other means to know himself, the Word of God, and through him the Father.
>
> He deals with them as a good teacher with his students, coming down to their level and using simple means. St. Paul says as much: "Since, in the wisdom of God, the world did not know God through wisdom, God decided, through the foolishness of our proclamation, to save those who believe" [1 Cor. 1:21 NRSV]. Humans had turned from the contemplation of God above, and were looking for him in the opposite direction, down among created and sense-perceptible things. The Savior of us all, the Word of God, in his great love took to himself a body and moved as Human among humans, meeting their senses, so to speak, halfway. He became himself an object for the senses, so that those who were seeking God in sense-perceptible things might apprehend the Father through the works which he, the Word of God, did in the body.[15]

Thus by seeing what Christ says and does as human, people can come to perceive that this is God in action. This perception will enable them to recognize God's presence and activity in other places too, and, as Athanasius says, through knowing the Son they will come to know the Father as well. Their bodily eyes that see the Savior will be more reliable than their unstable

15. *On the Incarnation* 14–15; trans. Anonymous, *St. Athanasius*, 42–43, alt.

imaginings. And as they perceive God made flesh, they will become aware of their own fallibility and thus guard themselves against delusion.

In this way, God reawakens our buried capacity to see spiritual reality. As fallen people, we thought the things we could see and touch physically, or maybe the products of our own imagination, were the whole of reality; so Christ came to us as a physical being we could see and touch. In seeing him, we could recognize that he was more than what we could perceive with our bodily eyes and greater than our mental fantasies. So we could begin to look deeper or farther, to perceive the spiritual realm. And once we had recognized God in Christ, we could begin to see God present in our neighbors and God at work throughout the material world.

Seeing People Truly

Two teenagers went to a reception for a famous pianist who performed concerts around the world and made many recordings. Dressed in jeans and T-shirts, these teens looked out of place, so someone was about to usher them out. Seeing this, the pianist came up to them and engaged them in conversation. He asked, "What is your name? What are you interested in? Do you play an instrument?" They talked for some time. One of the teenagers was so moved by this attention that he remembered the pianist fondly after he grew up. The other guests saw only the scruffy clothes, but the pianist saw eager young people interested in music. These teens may have seen in the pianist the image of God.

Once we come to know God, we will perceive his character, that is, his gentleness, patience, generosity, wisdom, justice, and love. Then we will slowly begin to recognize the divine character in people we meet, to see in them the divine image and likeness. Our appreciation and thankfulness will spread from God to our neighbors as we see the same good qualities in our neighbors that we found in God.

On the other hand, we may perceive gentleness, patience, generosity, wisdom, justice, or love in people first and so find the courage to believe that God is like such people, only even better. The author of 1 John says, "He who does not love his brother whom he has seen, cannot love God whom he has not seen" (4:20). I am thankful to those who manifest the image of God in their character and actions, because they make it easier for me to find and know God.

The tendency today, and maybe throughout history, is to see only what is bad in people, to be irritated with them, to complain, and to gossip. Yet if we can see that the surface annoyances are like masks in the theater, behind which is God's image, we will be like the pianist who saw the scruffy teenagers as potential lifelong music lovers. We will be moved to value our neighbors, to respect them, and even to love them.

The fathers and mothers of the desert perceived God through prayer, so they loved their neighbors, who were made in his image. They were realistic about the difficulties of loving people in practice, and their stories show how they saw their neighbors and persisted in laboring to love them. Their ability to discern people's real motivations and needs grew out of their love for people and their ability to see more than what appears on the surface. Abba Poemen's advice about how to rebuke sinners is a good example: "If a man sins and denies it, saying, 'I have not sinned,' do not correct him, or you will destroy any intention he might have of changing. If you say, 'Do not be cast down, my brother, but be careful about that in the future,' you will move his heart to repent."[16] Poemen understood that the erring monk would feel hurt when accused of sin. His hurt would move him to deny it and then make him unwilling to change, because he would prove his accuser right if he changed. The one who encourages him, however, treats him as a brother and gently turns his attention to future actions, thus moving him to repent. He will feel loved by his brother and will want to change for his brother's sake. Poemen's compassion for the

---

16. Translated in Ward, *Desert Fathers*, 100.

erring monk's pain surely helped him draw these wise and kind conclusions.

Abba Achillas, a craftsman who made ropes, showed similar wisdom and compassion when a group of three brothers came to him. Each had the same request, but his answers were different and responded to their differing personal needs:

> Three monks came to Achillas, and one of them had a bad reputation. The first monk said, "Abba, make me a fishing net." He said, "I won't." The second said to him, "Will you give us a memento of yourself to keep in our community?" He answered, "I don't have time." Then the third, the one with the bad reputation, said to him, "Make me a fishing net, and so I shall have a blessing from your hands, abba." At once he answered, "I will do that." But the first two, whose requests he had refused, said privately to him, "Why did you refuse our requests and consent to his?" Achillas answered, "I could tell you that I would not do it because I had no time, and you would not be troubled. But if I did not do it for this monk, he would say, 'The hermit has heard of my reputation and for that reason has refused to make me a net.' So immediately I set to work with the string, to soothe his soul and prevent him being sad."[17]

Achillas surely sees that people are in the habit of expecting bad things from the monk they have labeled with a bad reputation. That monk has come to expect that they will discriminate against him again and again, so naturally he feels hurt and alienated in his community. Achillas takes the time to give the man a fishing net he can take with him and keep as an expression of appreciation and support.

Yet the desert fathers and mothers also saw evil and faced it honestly. They grieved when they saw people committing sins, which damaged the divine image in those people and often hurt others too. They prayed that God would lead sinners away from their destructive habits and prepare them for eternal life in his kingdom.

17. Translated in Ward, *Desert Fathers*, 91, alt.

Abba Ammonas, a desert monk who knew Anthony, was made a bishop. He fulfilled his pastoral and administrative duties but continued in his monastic way of life. Bishops in the ancient world were often powerful aristocrats. They had the task of judging Christians who had committed serious sins and assigning penances, that is, works such as prayer and fasting that the sinner would have to do in order to be readmitted to full participation in the church community. When people brought sinners to Ammonas, accusing them and asking him to judge them, he responded with insight and compassion. As a man of prayer, he could see who the sinners really were as well as the context of their lives, regardless of what they had done wrong. One case involved a young teenaged girl who had become pregnant. She was vulnerable in a world without modern medicine, a world where women in childbirth and their babies often died. She was a social outcast in the village and was poor and sick. Some self-righteous Christians, maybe monks who were scandalized by her sexual sin, brought her to Bishop Ammonas.

> Someone brought a young girl who was pregnant to him, saying, "See what this unhappy wretch has done; give her a penance." But he, having marked the young girl's womb with the sign of the cross [as a blessing], commanded that six pairs of fine linen sheets should be given her, saying, "It is for fear that, when she comes to give birth, she may die, she or the child, and have nothing for the burial." But her accusers resumed, "Why did you do that? Give her a punishment." But he said to them, "Look, brothers, she is near to death; what am I to do?" Then he sent her away, and no old man dared accuse anyone any more.[18]

If she died in childbirth, she would be wrapped in the linen sheets as a shroud and then buried, as would the baby if it died. In the early church, sinners on their deathbeds would be forgiven the rest of their penances and readmitted to communion so they could be prepared to meet God. This is prob-

---

18. Ammonas 8; trans. Ward, *Sayings*, 27.

ably what Ammonas, in his compassion, foresaw. It would have been inappropriate to punish the vulnerable young girl at that point. Desert monks took sexual sins very seriously, and they often had a low opinion of women, who could be an occasion of temptations for them. Ammonas saw the girl for the human being she was and cut through all the judgment and prejudice that surrounded her.

On another occasion, he, like Abba Achillas, encountered a monk with a bad reputation. He also responded with compassion, although this brother was hiding a woman in his living quarters:

> Abba Ammonas came one day to eat in a place where there was a monk of evil repute. Now it happened that a woman came and entered the cell of the brother of evil reputation. The dwellers in that place, having learnt this, were troubled and gathered together to chase the brother from his cell. Knowing that Bishop Ammonas was in the place, they asked him to join them. When the brother in question learnt this, he hid the woman in a large barrel. The crowd of monks came to the place. Now Abba Ammonas saw the position clearly but for the sake of God he kept the secret; he entered, seated himself on the barrel and commanded the cell to be searched. Then, when the monks had searched everywhere without finding the woman, Abba Ammonas said, "What is this? May God forgive you!" After praying, he made everyone go out, then, taking the brother by the hand, he said, "Brother, be on your guard." With these words, he withdrew.[19]

The other monks intended to throw the sinful brother out of the community, but Ammonas stopped them. He saw to it that they were publicly embarrassed for accusing the sinner, rebuked them, and asked them to leave the accused brother's cell. Then, like Abba Poemen, he gave the sinner a gentle warning about the future instead of accusing him directly. His wise and discreet actions moved everyone involved toward healing.

19. Ammonas 10; trans. Ward, *Sayings*, 28.

Anthony the Great, father of the desert monks, said, "Our life and our death are with our neighbor. If we do good to our neighbor, we do good to God; if we cause our neighbor to stumble, we sin against Christ."[20] Poemen, Achillas, and Ammonas could see the divine image in people they met, both those who imitated God's virtues and those who sinned. So, like God, they acted toward their neighbors with dignity and kindness.

Like the brothers in the desert, people today know others who have set good examples they can follow or who have served as mentors. These may be parents, teachers, grandparents, pastors, or good neighbors and friends. By word or example, they provide models of how best to live. Remembering their example can protect us from going astray. Let us each give thanks for those we have been privileged to know, because through them we can see God present in his image and likeness.

20. Translated in Ward, *Desert Fathers*, 177.

4

Virtues and Humility

As a child I asked myself, "Can I really do good? Can I make a positive contribution to the lives of other people? Can I become a good person?" Many of the adults surrounding me told me I was bad. As a child I kept asking myself about becoming good but did not dare ask others because I knew nobody would give me an honest, helpful answer. I was alone with my questions. I wonder how many people today find themselves in a similar situation? An important part of the good news of Jesus Christ is that human beings can become good and can do good for others, because God will help them.

One of the most memorable leaders among the fourth-century Egyptian desert fathers was Abba Moses the Black. Before he became a monk, and especially afterward, he probably asked himself the same questions about becoming good and doing good for others. Moses lived in Egypt but came from sub-Saharan Africa, and as a young man he was a slave. In the Greco-Roman world, there were many slaves, but they did not necessarily belong to any particular race. The Egyptians, however, were prejudiced against black people. Moses endured

ridicule from other monks because of his color. He was grieved
but kept silent about it.[1]

Moses was tall and physically strong. As a young man, he
ran away from his owner and became the leader of a group
of fierce highway robbers. He lived with them in the wilder-
ness for years, and there was talk that he may have committed
murder.[2] At some point, maybe because he was in danger of
being caught, though we do not know the reason, he went to
the large monastic settlement of Scetis and became a monk.
He took to heart the monastic values, put them into practice—
which meant completely changing his way of life—and later
became a leader of the community. Shortly after he joined,
some robbers came to his cell to steal from him. In his former
life, he would have killed them, and he was still strong enough
to catch them all. Palladius, a fifth-century historian, tells
what happened:

> Four robbers, not knowing who he was, attacked him in his cell.
> He tied them all together like a package, put them on his back
> like a bundle of straw, and took them to the monastic church.
> "Since I must not hurt anyone," he said, "what do you want me
> to do with these men?" The robbers confessed [their attempted
> crime] and knew that he was Moses, the onetime notorious and
> well-known robber. They glorified God and renounced the world
> [to become monks] because of his conversion. For they reasoned
> in this way: "If he who was such a strong and powerful thief
> fears God, why should we put off our own salvation?"[3]

When the monastic elders told Moses to let the robbers go,
and he did so, they were moved to become monks by the community's respect for their humanity and forbearance toward
their crime.

Moses, who once retaliated with vengeance against anyone
who offended him, became renowned for his humility and his

1. Moses 3; trans. Ward, *Sayings*, 139.
2. Palladius, *Lausiac History* 19.1; trans. Meyer, *Palladius*, 67.
3. *Lausiac History* 19.4–5; trans. Meyer, *Palladius*, 68, alt.

forgiveness of others. His refusal to judge is illustrated in the following story of a meeting called to punish a monk who had sinned:

> A brother at Scetis committed a fault. A council was called to which Abba Moses was invited, but he refused to go to it. Then the priest sent someone to say to him, "Come, for everyone is waiting for you." So he got up and went. He took a leaking jug, filled it with water and carried it with him [on his back]. The others came out to meet him and said to him, "What is this, father?" The old man said to them, "My sins run out behind me, and I do not see them, and today I am coming to judge the errors of another." When they heard that, they said no more to the brother but forgave him.[4]

Moses acted out a parable like the Hebrew prophets of old. He must never have forgotten the sins he committed as a highway robber, and he was mindful too of sins he committed every day as a monk. So in compassion and love, he forgave others. "When someone is occupied with his own faults," he said, "he does not see those of his neighbor."[5]

Moses was also renowned for his hospitality. He treated guests with such kindness and generosity that he often had monks visiting his cell. He delighted in their company, and they delighted in his. It was as if when they talked, he was sharing honey cakes with angels.[6] When he was a robber, his relationships with neighbors would have been hostile, but his earlier hostility was now transformed into love.

He died as a martyr when foreigners attacked Scetis. They killed him with a sword, and he refused to run away or defend himself, since he said that in his youth he had killed with a sword. When brothers asked him to flee, he quoted Jesus, who said, "All who take the sword will perish by the sword" (Matt. 26:52).[7]

4. Moses 2; trans. Ward, *Sayings*, 138–39.
5. Instructions Abba Moses sent to Abba Poemen 3; trans. Ward, *Sayings*, 141.
6. Arsenius 38; trans. Ward, *Sayings*, 18.
7. Moses 10; trans. Ward, *Sayings*, 140.

With God's help, Moses was transformed by accepting the guidance of his elders at Scetis and exerting persistent, long-term effort. In this way, his sin was changed to repentance, his vengeance to forgiveness, his hostility to hospitality, and his fierceness to kindness and gentleness. The criminal became a saint, able in turn to help many others. The Holy Spirit, together with experienced desert spiritual guides, taught him in practice how to become a good person and do good for others.

Virtue as Image and Likeness of God

I have observed in monasteries today how monks and nuns take care not to gossip about other's failings. Instead, they admire and discuss what people have done right, often in difficult circumstances. They may see a mother advocating persistently with health-care providers to get her child needed care or a man doing excellent work for a troublesome boss without growing resentful. Then the monks or nuns ask themselves and each other, "How did they do it? Can I learn from their example?"

Early Christian writers are also very interested in good character. Their writings, especially their sermons, are full of reflection about virtues. Like today's monks and nuns, they seek to analyze how people do good, and then look for examples that they and their congregations can follow. Yet modern readers are sometimes bored by this kind of writing. People today are often put off even by the word *virtue*. It makes them think of their fussy, Victorian grandmothers scolding them for using the salad fork for the main course at a dinner party. Does virtue matter in our complex world?

Maybe which fork you use does not make much difference, but how people treat one another does matter. When members of Congress try to score political points against the other party instead of working together to pass legislation that the entire country needs, resentments build, grudges are kept, and the atmosphere of public discourse is poisoned. When companies calculate that they can make more money by slashing customer service because all their competitors are doing the same thing, everybody's quality of life deteriorates and nobody takes responsibility for resolving problems. So maybe good character is important after all.

By *virtue*, people in the Greco-Roman world, including Christians, meant something more than table manners. The word *arete*, which is usually translated "virtue," means excellence of action, habits, and especially character. The virtues recognized by philosophers like Plato include things like wisdom, moderation, courage, and justice. Christians added to this list such qualities as humility, repentance, forgiveness, faith, hope, and love. All these qualities are still attractive today. We appreciate them when we see them in others, and we may strive to practice them ourselves. Finally, God possesses these kinds of characteristics, and Christ lived them in a human context. God has shown that the virtues are indeed God's glory. They are truly more precious than gold. As John Chrysostom said in the sermon quoted at the beginning of chapter 3, virtues are true, lasting wealth that a person can carry into the next life, where all the riches of this world are gone.

The sixth-century abbot Dorotheus of Gaza believes that virtues are natural to us as human persons. This belief may seem counterintuitive; it is easy to slide into sin, but virtues require persistent effort. Yet Dorotheus's view of virtues represents the theology of the Greek Christian writers. Dorotheus cites Scripture to explain his belief:

> By God's gift the virtues belong to the nature we possess. For truly when God made man he sowed the virtues in him, as it says: "Let us make man in our image, after our likeness" [Gen. 1:26 RSV]. To his image, since God made the soul incorruptible and self-determining; to his likeness, which means having similar virtues. Does the scripture not say: "Be merciful, even as your Father is merciful" [Luke 6:36 RSV]? And: "Be holy, for I am holy" [Lev. 11:44 RSV]? And again, the apostle says, "Be kind to one another" [Eph. 4:32 RSV]. In the Psalm: "The Lord

is kind to those who wait for him" [Lam. 3:25 RSV, alt.]. There are more like these, each showing this likeness to God. God gave us the virtues as an endowment of our nature.[8]

Notice how Dorotheus makes a distinction between God's image and likeness. For him, the image includes self-determination, which is the freedom we discussed in chapter 1. It also includes the soul's immortality, which is an image of God's eternity. For writers like Dorotheus, who distinguish the likeness from the image, the likeness is generally greater than the image. It consists primarily in human virtues similar to those of God. Here Dorotheus lists several that are found in Scripture: mercy, holiness, and kindness. His list is not exhaustive. He notes that there are other divine virtues as well. There is a great abundance, a variety of virtues, and together they manifest the different facets of God's splendid character.

As noted in chapter 1, Basil of Caesarea also distinguishes between image and likeness. He says, "By our creation we have the first, and by our free choice we build the second." Through our freedom, God "has made us with the power to become like God." That is, besides being free by nature, we humans have from God the ability to acquire all the virtues. Interestingly, Basil sums up acquiring God's likeness, or the virtues, as "becoming Christian."[9] By this he means living in a Christian way throughout one's lifetime. He goes on to explain what he means, and like Dorotheus he quotes Scripture:

"Become perfect as your heavenly Father is perfect" [Matt. 5:48, my translation]. Do you see how the Lord restores to us that which is according to the likeness? "For he makes his sun rise on the evil and on the good, and sends rain on the just and on the unjust" [Matt. 5:45 RSV]. If you become a hater of evil, free of rancor, not remembering yesterday's enmity; if you

8. *Discourse* 12; trans. Wheeler, *Dorotheos of Gaza*, 188, alt. Dorotheus appears to have confused Psalms and Lamentations here, a minor slip of memory. Many early Christians, especially monks, quoted the Scriptures from memory.
9. *On the Origin of Humanity* 1.16; trans. Harrison, *St. Basil*, 43–44.

become brother-loving and compassionate, you are like God. If you forgive your enemy from your heart, you are like God. If as God is toward you, the sinner, you become the same toward the brother who has wronged you, by your good will from your heart toward your neighbor, you are like God. As you have that which is according to the image through your being rational, you come to be according to the likeness by undertaking kindness. Take on yourself "a heart of compassion, kindness," that you may put on Christ.[10]

Thus by "putting on Christ," by becoming united with him, one is enabled to share in his virtues.

Virtues are the free gift of God and Christ to us. So in the first place, they belong to God. This means that even though exercising the virtues is human nature, it is not enough for us to work at acquiring them ourselves. Just as we receive other aspects of the divine image—such as life, light, and perception of God—as God's gifts, the same is true of virtues. This is because it is our nature as human persons to be in relationship with God. Even when we do not know the source of the gift, it is God who enables us to become fully human.

Gregory of Nyssa's understanding is similar to Basil's. He draws a parallel between God's many names, which describe God's good qualities, and the many virtues that belong to human beings. Just as God has many different characteristics—such as wisdom, moderation, and justice—yet is one God, so people are called to have many diverse virtues, yet the virtues all work together to form a single excellent character.[11]

Gregory says that Christ, who as God was beyond our understanding, became incarnate as the "image of the invisible God" (Col. 1:15) so that he could be a model for human beings, an example for them to imitate. People can then be like students in an art class in which a fine painting is set before them and they each have the task of copying it on their own canvases, attempting to bring forth the same beauty in their own

10. *On the Origin of Humanity* 1.17; trans. Harrison, *St. Basil*, 44, alt.
11. *On the Beatitudes* 4.5; trans. Hall, "Gregory of Nyssa," 52–53.

art. Gregory says that likewise "every person is the painter of his own life, and choice is the craftsman of the work, and the virtues are the paints for producing the image."[12] If we paint well, we become an image of Christ, who is the image of the Father,[13] "as did Paul, who became an 'imitator of Christ' [see 1 Cor. 11:1] through his life of virtue."[14] Thus we are called to use our freedom to choose Christ as our model and to produce his likeness in ourselves. The virtues are a crucial part in this process. They are like the paints themselves, which portray his likeness in us.

The artistic work of copying such a model requires effort, skill, concentration, and precision. It is easy to mess up the paints through our faulty character and actions, making their colors muddy instead of beautiful, and to depict an ugly picture instead of disclosing Christ's beauty. When we sin, we make a mess instead of revealing the likeness of God. We also separate ourselves from Christ, as our will turns aside from his will.

In the next paragraph, Gregory switches from the metaphor of a painting class to Paul's metaphor of Christ as the head and humankind as his body. A continuity exists between the head and the body so that "whatever the head is by nature, this the individual parts become, in order to be in communion with the head."[15] So while it is necessary for the parts to imitate the head in order to remain connected to it, the head is the source of the virtues present in the parts. That is, Christ, and not just our own effort, is the source of the virtues present in those who imitate him. Gregory adds that in a human body, the movement toward action begins in the head—today we would say in the brain—and then the hands or feet carry out the action. Likewise, when we choose to carry out Christ's will we remain joined to him, and he then enables us to act in ways that make us like

12. *On Perfection*; trans. Callahan, *Gregory of Nyssa*, 110.
13. Remember that Gregory of Nyssa does not make a distinction between image and likeness.
14. *On Perfection*; trans. Callahan, *Gregory of Nyssa*, 111.
15. *On Perfection*; trans. Callahan, *Gregory of Nyssa*, 112.

him.[16] Thus, just as he would refuse to react to insulting words, he enables us also to forgive those who insult us.

In another work, Gregory again uses the analogy of painting to speak about the divine likeness in the human person. But here God is the painter, not our free choice. We can conclude that since both God and we are engaged in the task of producing our character, what is needed is a synergy, or a cooperation, between God's creativity and our freedom. Here is what Gregory says:

> Painters transfer human forms to their pictures by using certain colored paints. They put on their copy the proper and corresponding shades, so that the beauty of the original may be accurately transferred to the likeness. Similarly, understand that when painting an image of his own beauty, our Maker also shows us his own sovereignty by adding virtues as if they were colors. In the image, the colors, so to speak, by which the form is portrayed, are manifold and varied.[17]

These shades are not the colors of the human face—red, white, or the flesh tone that comes from blending them—nor the black of eye and eyebrow, "but instead of these, purity, freedom from unruly emotion, blessedness, alienation from all evil, and all things like these, through which the likeness of God is formed in the human being. With such hues the Fashioner of his own image stamped our nature."[18]

For Gregory, God is the Creator of the divine image in the human person at the beginning and continues to create the divine image and likeness in us throughout our lives as we grow in the virtues. Of course, for this to happen we must choose to become like God, or Christ, and we must be willing to use the virtues given us. And as Gregory says, these gifts of virtue are many and varied.

16. On Perfection; trans. Callahan, Gregory of Nyssa, 112–13.
17. On the Making of Humanity 5.1; PG 44:137A–B; trans. Moore and Wilson, Gregory, 391, alt.
18. On the Making of Humanity 5.1; PG 44:137B; trans. Moore and Wilson, Gregory, 391, alt.

Virtues and Passions

Since God has endowed us with virtues, and since they are natural to us as human persons, why do we find it so hard to live a life of virtue? Abba Moses showed in his life as a monk that he had the capacity for forgiveness of others, for hospitality, and for gentleness. Yet in his youth he was filled with fierceness and vengeance toward others. As a human being, he had the ability to love his neighbors, but this love had been transformed into hostility. His used his natural skill with people to lead a gang of robbers, though later in life he applied the same talent to his work as a priest and leader of the monastic community. His youth is an example of how our human capacities and energies can become twisted and misdirected so that instead of practicing virtues we commit sins. Yet Moses always had in him the raw material for forgiveness, hospitality, and gentleness, even when he was misusing it. As a monk he was taught, and slowly learned, how to reorient his talents and energies toward love for God and neighbor.

To understand how this works, let us briefly consider the psychology of the early Greek Christians. They believed that the soul gives life to the body, yet it also contains mental and emotional capacities, including reason and free choice. So the soul experiences emotions, such as fear and desire, sorrow and joy. Plato worked out a three-part model of the soul that became standard in the popular philosophy of Late Antiquity and in much of the Eastern Christian tradition of spiritual psychology. It is important to understand that although this model names distinct activities or "parts" of the human person that interact in various ways, it is only a model. The "parts" it names are not separate, self-enclosed, static entities that form components of the self. Rather, each person is a whole that moves in various directions and reacts to his or her environment in various ways.

The first and highest of the soul's three "parts" or capacities is reason, mind, or intellect. This intellect is understood to be greater, deeper, and broader than the "reasoning brain" emphasized today. Its activities include not only cognition and reasoning but also moral insight, deliberation, and freedom of choice. The intellect perceives the material world through the senses and organizes and evaluates these perceptions. Yet its highest and most important function is to perceive spiritual realities, including other people, angels, and ultimately God. According to Basil, the mind can be used for good, evil, or morally neutral purposes, depending on where it focuses its attention and for what purposes. For example, it can gaze toward the true God, which is good, or it can invent and worship idols. The mind can also learn and practice various skills, like being an airline pilot or a doctor. These skills, according to Basil, are morally neutral in themselves, but they can be used for good or evil purposes.[19] A pilot can bring passengers safely to their destination, yet he also knows how to crash his plane into a New York skyscraper resulting in great loss of life.

In a mature, well-balanced human life, our intellect is supposed to discern, receive, and obey the will of God and to guide and bring order to the other two "parts" of the soul, which are understood to include the instinctive and emotional impulses and drives. So emotions like desire and anger are supposed to follow the mind's discernment, not the other way around. The mind is like the driver of a cart, while the emotional impulses are like the two horses. If the driver lets the horses run away with the cart, it will crash. This is, in effect, what happens when people use their intellects to invent a lot of unnecessary new possessions to desire or multiply anger by devising clever ways to get revenge on enemies. Yet when reason is in charge, driver and horses work together. With the horses, the driver gets where he is going much more quickly than if he walked without the horses. We can reject evil and love and serve God and our neighbors much better with the energy of our emotions than without it.

Like the mind, both of the nonrational impulses can be used for good or for evil purposes, depending on which direction they turn and move. One of these impulses is desire, which

19. *Letter* 233; trans. Harrison, *St. Basil*, 107–9.

seeks either to move a person toward various things or persons or to draw those things or persons toward the self. When misdirected, desire is obsessively focused on the wrong things, yet it also serves as the necessary driving force in love for God and love for neighbor.

The other nonrational impulse is called *thymos* in Greek, a word that is difficult to translate. This impulse complements desire in that it pushes things away from the self and sets limits on other impulses, one's own or those of other people. Well-ordered *thymos* can be a useful ally to reason in curbing one's inordinate desires, like a loyal soldier who has left his weapons with his wise general (reason) and is ready to serve at his commander's bidding.[20] *Thymos* is also the necessary driving force at work in virtues like perseverance, courage, self-restraint, rejection of evil, and struggle for justice. Yet it is most closely associated with anger, and in some contexts this is what *thymos* means, though it clearly has a broader range of meanings. Perhaps one of the best English translations of *thymos* is "assertiveness," which is different from aggression.

When a person's life is rightly ordered, all these impulses and drives work together harmoniously to serve virtue. This is because they are guided by reason and obedient to God's will. This harmony, however, has become disrupted in humankind's fallen condition. Our soul's impulses pull us in different directions and are often in conflict with each other. Yet early Christians were well aware that the emotions are given to us by our Creator for good purposes and that the mind also can be sinfully misused. Thus the whole person turns toward God, turns away from him in sin, or turns back toward him in repentance. When human reason and emotions are again directed toward God, the harmony for which God created them is restored. Much early Christian preaching aims to lead us toward this restoration.

In Greek Christian spirituality, the opposite of virtues are called "passions." This is a technical term and has a different meaning from the same word in contemporary English. For

20. Basil, *Homily against Anger* 5; trans. Harrison, *St. Basil*, 88–89.

example, when someone says, "I have a passion for serving the poor," he or she is talking about a virtue, not a sin. In Greek Christian spirituality, passions are instincts or emotions that are misdirected and therefore pull us away from God. They are actually temptations, not sins. Almost everybody, however holy, will experience thoughts coming into the mind or moods that come and go. The sin comes when one focuses one's attention on the tempting thoughts or the bad mood. Then it colors one's whole state of mind, and one is eventually moved to act on it. For example, Adam sees the forbidden fruit, notices it is attractive, and desires it. He could easily turn away at this point and put the fruit out of his mind. At first his desire is a small thing, significant but easily overcome. If he were to turn away at this point, no sin would be committed. But instead, he gazes at the fruit, reflects on how delicious it must be, and imagines eating it. His desire to taste it grows and becomes very hard to resist. So he takes it and eats it.

In the fourth century, Evagrius Ponticus built the insights of the Egyptian desert into a synthetic picture of the soul—its virtues and passions—that has been standard in the Eastern church to this day. His understanding of the three "parts" of the soul, and the passions and virtues pertaining to each one, can be summarized as follows:[21]

Passions and Virtues in the Soul

Parts of soul	Passions	Virtues
intellect	vainglory	prudence
	pride	understanding
		wisdom
assertiveness	restless boredom	perseverance
	anger	courage
	sadness, depression	self-restraint

21. My account of the three parts of the soul and the eight passionate thoughts draws from Bamberger, *Evagrius Ponticus*; Roberta Bondi, *To Love as God Loves* (Philadelphia: Fortress, 1987), 57–77; and William Harmless, *Desert Christians: An Introduction to the Literature of Early Monasticism* (Oxford: Oxford University Press, 2004), 311–71.

Parts of soul	Passions	Virtues
desire	gluttony	continence
	fornication	moderation
	love of money	love

The eight passions listed in the second column are those
Evagrius names as most important, though there are certainly
others as well. We can twist good into evil in any number of
ways. The virtues in the right column are not an exhaustive list
either, since God, who practices them and has formed them
in people, is endlessly creative. There are always new ways of
becoming good, doing good, and sharing in God's activities.
Yet this table suggests how our natural impulses are most easily
misdirected into passions and which virtues our passions can
become when they are reoriented according to the divine will.

Vainglory is an obsession with what other people think of
me. Pride is the thought that I, and not God, am the source of
my own virtues and talents. To see my weaknesses and recognize
God as the source of my talents is the beginning of prudence,
understanding, and wisdom. Prudence is insight about practical situations in life and leads one to see things in proportion
and act appropriately. Understanding is intellectual mastery,
the fruit of learning. Wisdom is deep, abiding insight about the
meanings of Scripture, about virtues and vices, and about God
and spiritual realities.

Restless boredom, or listlessness, is a widespread unrecog-
nized problem today. It makes a person hate present circumstances and long to move elsewhere and do other things. The
anger in this list of passions is actually hostility toward others,
not the anger that is used constructively, say, to work for justice.
Sadness can equally be called depression; it makes everything
look useless, colorless, and meaningless. Restless boredom and
depression result when a person gives up on being constructively
assertive, while anger is misdirected assertiveness (*thymos*).
When we choose to be assertive in constructive ways, we break
the chains of restless boredom and sadness. The results of our
assertiveness will then be perseverance in the face of obstacles,

courage in the face of threats, and self-restraint when tempted to stray from seeking the goals of wholeness in God's kingdom and of justice on earth. The last three passions are obsessive desires that get in the way of healthy family life, valuing and sharing God's creation, and eating to live rather than living to eat. When we turn our attention away from these obsessions and toward God, our desire becomes the driving force of our spiritual life. We can look back with moderation and continence at the things we once desired. As we love God, we will come to see God present and active in our neighbors and in the created world around us, and we will love them also.

If we are honest, we will each realize that we are familiar with all these passions from our own experience. We all have the task of collaborating with God to work and struggle with our passions until they become virtues and manifest his likeness. Gregory of Nyssa explains that this happens when the soul's original balance is restored and our intellect, guided by God, guides the emotions toward harmony.

> If reason receives back control over such emotions, each of them is transformed into a kind of virtue. For anger produces courage, cowardice produces steadiness, fear produces obedience, hatred produces turning away from evil, the power of love produces the desire for what is truly beautiful [i.e., God]. Haughtiness in our character raises our thought above the passions and protects it from bondage to evil. Yes, even the great apostle praises such a form of uplifting when he directs us to "set your minds" constantly "on things that are above" [Col. 3:2 RSV]. And so one finds that every such movement, when lifted up by loftiness of mind, is conformed to the beauty of the divine image.[22]

Gregory is saying that even eros can become love for God, and even the impulse toward pride, which is the worst of sins, can be turned into a habit of looking down on temptations and sins so

---

22. *On the Creation of Humanity* 18.5; PG 44.193B–C; trans. Moore and Wilson, *Gregory*, 406, alt.

as to avoid them while looking up toward God. So he makes the bold claim that every one of our misdirected emotions can be redirected toward that for which God originally created it. And then it has become a virtue and manifests God's likeness. This claim is grounded in the spiritual psychology described above. The human capacities of intellect, assertiveness, and desire remain the same. But their energies are redirected in a way that furthers harmony within the self and love for God and neighbor. These human capacities and energies are intrinsic to who we are. Passions become virtues when the energies of intellect and emotion, assertiveness and desire are redirected and used for good purposes.

Humility

How is a Christian to practice virtues and overcome passions? This is an all-encompassing question that was of great concern to early Christians. Virtually all the early Christian sermons we have, all the stories of the desert, and much of the rest of early Christian literature aim to answer this question. It would take a whole volume, probably many volumes, to summarize such vast material. So instead I will focus on one virtue that is not on Evagrius's list but is central to early Christian spirituality and is the foundation of all other virtues, namely, humility. As the Cistercian abbot André Louf says, humility is "an all-encompassing virtue—the heart of stone shattered and restored to life as the heart of flesh—the virtue from which all other virtues are derived."[23] There is also testimony from the greatest of the desert fathers: "Abba Anthony said, 'I saw all the snares of the enemy spread out over the world, and I said groaning, "What can get me through such snares?" Then I heard a voice saying to me, "Humility.""[24]

Another leader of the desert monks learned something similar:

23. André Louf, *The Way of Humility*, trans. Lawrence S. Cunningham (Kalamazoo, MI: Cistercian Publications, 2007), 21.
24. Anthony 7; trans. Ward, *Sayings*, 2, alt.

When Abba Macarius was returning from the marsh to his cell one day carrying some palm leaves, he met the devil on the road with a scythe. The [devil] struck at him as much as he pleased, but in vain, and he said to him, "What is your power, Macarius, that makes me powerless against you? All that you do, I do too; you fast, so do I; you keep vigil, and I do not sleep at all; in one thing only do you beat me." Abba Macarius asked what this was. He said, "Your humility. Because of that I can do nothing against you."[25]

In this story, Macarius goes about his daily work. He has to get palm leaves to make them into baskets to sell. Many of the Egyptian desert monks at that time did this so they could buy food for themselves and have something left over to give to the needy. The devil meets him on the road and attacks him but can do him no harm. Being a bodiless spirit, he can boast that he does everything the monks do, only better, things such as going without food and sleep. Then craftily he entices Macarius to ask what he has that the devil lacks, and the answer is humility. So here is a temptation for Macarius to be proud of his humility, which would destroy it. This story does not tell how, but the monk is wise enough to recognize and avoid this snare. As a humble monk, he relies continually on God's help instead of his own strength and thus is protected from the devil's attacks.

According to the desert elders, the acquisition of humility is a crucial turning point in the spiritual journey. Yet it is very difficult to write about. In the first place, who is qualified to write about it? Louf addresses this question in the introduction to his book:

What right do I have to speak about humility? Am I to consider myself as an expert on this topic? Or do I set myself up as an example? Who would dare make such a claim since, at the same time, it would be clear proof that one totally lacked humility? "To assert that one is not proud," says Saint John Climacus, "is

25. Macarius 11; trans. Ward, *Sayings*, 129–30.

one of the clearest proofs that one is proud."[26] To believe oneself
to be humble is still worse. It leaves one open to ridicule.[27]

These words apply to me more than to André Louf, who is
an experienced monk and abbot. Yet before discussing the royal
dignity of the human person in chapter 5, then more about the
powers and responsibilities of those made in God's image, it is
necessary to discuss humility. Without humility the virtues cannot be rightly practiced nor human dignity truthfully affirmed
nor virtuous deeds authentically accomplished. To do these
things arrogantly would undermine the work itself and would
separate the human person from God, the source of life. Arrogant virtues would become vices, and arrogant deeds would
not show the likeness of God, who is supremely humble.

Further, it is difficult to speak about humility today without
being misunderstood. Unfortunately, humility has often been
used falsely as a weapon to keep women, the disabled, and
members of minority groups in "their place" and to silence
their righteous protests by labeling them as proud, supposedly
in the name of Christ. Such oppression cannot be humble; it
points the finger at others and puts them down, allegedly for
the purpose of making *them* humble. True humility does the
opposite: it always looks at how the self is acting and does not
judge others but quietly leads by example. Yet the concept has
been abused so much that, as Roberta Bondi says, to speak of
humility as early Christians did "will be repulsive, especially
to women and minorities who have had to struggle for their
own self-esteem as well as their place in the world and even in
the church."[28]

Real humility has nothing to do with creating in myself a low
self-image or making myself feel guilty. It means recognizing
that all my talents and virtues are gifts from God, gifts for which
I am profoundly thankful. These gifts are entrusted to me so
I can share them with people around me. I also share in their

26. *The Ladder of Divine Ascent*, step 23.
27. Louf, *Way of Humility*, 3.
28. Bondi, *Love as God Loves*, 43.

gifts, for which I am thankful to those people and to God. Real humility is also a recognition in practice that God loves each of my neighbors just as he loves me, so each one is invaluable. Humility is not about pondering how awful I think I am. It is about how I relate to others. Because the patterns of human relationships are structured differently today than they were in late antique Roman society, humility will often be practiced differently today than the ways ancient texts suggest. These texts were perhaps addressed to elite males, who had been told from childhood that they were models of excellence and were better than the people around them. So to restore balance, such men had to reflect on their lowliness.

Valerie Saiving argued in the 1960's that men need similar advice because they are taught by society to excel and to stand out from the crowd. She argues that women, by contrast, are often taught to be self-effacing and to sacrifice their needs for the sake of others. When this happens, Christianity, with its message of humility, reinforces the imbalance they have already learned. One cannot continually share oneself with others, or give oneself away, especially if one has no self left to give. This is a recipe for burnout; when burned out, one no longer has anything to give to others. So women need to find and affirm their true selves, recognize that they are distinct from others, and affirm that distinctness as okay.[29] Today, however, Saiving's suggestions do not apply only to women. Members of minority groups are probably in a similar situation to women. Moreover, the forward-looking abbot of a thriving monastic community has told me that many of the young white men who come there as novices have the same problem as Saiving's women.

To be humble is often understood to mean becoming a servant. One wonders what African-American women, who may be descended from generations of housemaids who lacked other career options, think of Christian exhortations to servanthood? As Letty Russell says, "Women and others in modern society

29. Valerie Saiving, "The Human Situation: A Feminine View," in *Womanspirit Rising: A Feminist Reader in Religion*, ed. Carol P. Christ and Judith Plaskow (San Francisco: HarperSanFrancisco, 1979, 1992), 25–42.

do not like the idea of servanthood because they see it as an expression of their own *powerlessness*."[30] Yet God is a servant and is certainly not powerless or ineffective. So women may prefer to speak of service as "social action" and of becoming "change agents"[31] who serve society in ways that bring much-needed justice. The aim is a kind of society in which "women are set free both to serve and be served without loss of identity or fear of subordination."[32]

This will happen for both genders when everyone practices genuine humility and those in leadership set the example for others to follow. Humility means honoring the divine image in other people and admitting one's own needs. It often means being willing to accept service from others. Many people find accepting service harder than giving service, which can easily be turned into a way of proving one's value as a human being while exerting power over others. With real humility, service simply addresses the neighbor's need with no ulterior motives because one no longer needs to prove one's value or accumulate power.

Acquiring Humility

How can people today become humble? One traditional way will probably not work: telling oneself over and over that one is the worst of sinners, that everyone else is better than oneself, that everyone will be saved except me; in fact, even nonrational beasts are better than me because they have not sinned and I have. Many people today, ground down by the hidden but persistent messages of contemporary society, are secretly terrified that these messages might be true of them. People today are tempted to depression and despair, more so than people were in Late Antiquity. Thinking thoughts about how worthless one is can be dangerous psychologically and spiritually and is to be

---

30. Letty M. Russell, *Human Liberation in a Feminist Perspective—A Theology* (Philadelphia: Westminster, 1974), 142, emphasis in the original.
31. Russell, *Human Liberation*, 142.
32. Russell, *Human Liberation*, 144.

avoided. Indeed, this book aims to show readers that all people have value before God.

How, then, can we acquire true humility as opposed to the false humility of simply putting oneself down? Let me suggest two ways, both present in early Christian sources. Basil of Caesarea suggests the first way. It involves maintaining a balance in one's opinion of oneself. When tempted either to pride or despair, one can think of the opposite side of the human condition and thus restore balance oneself. In other words, when exhilarated with limitless powers and possibilities, remember that one is made of dust; but when constrained and depressed, remember that one is made in God's image. Further, Basil recognizes that people's social class and economic condition influence their thinking, so he suggests different advice to the rich and to the poor. In both cases, the remedy is to "be attentive to yourself" (Deut. 15:9, my translation), to see things about yourself that you previously overlooked. Basil begins by summarizing both positions:

"Be attentive to yourself." This word is for you also when you are brilliantly successful, and all of your life is flowing like a stream. It is useful in protecting you as a kind of good adviser bringing a reminder of things human. And of course also when hard pressed by circumstances, on occasion you can sing it in your heart, so that you are neither lifted up by conceit to excessive pretension, nor give in to ignoble thoughts, falling into despair.[33]

Basil then exhorts the affluent and proud to remember their human lowliness:

Are you proud of wealth? And do you have grand thoughts about your ancestors? And do you exult in your homeland and bodily beauty and the honors given you by all? Be attentive to yourself, mindful that you are mortal, that "you are earth, and to earth you will return" [Gen. 3:19, my translation]. Look around, examining those of like eminence before you. Where are those who

---

33. *Homily on the Words "Be Attentive to Yourself"* 5; trans. Harrison, *St. Basil*, 100.

possessed civil authority? Where are the unconquerable orators? Where are the leaders of public assemblies, the brilliant horse breeders, the generals, the governors, the despots? Are they not all dust? Are they not all legend? Are not the memorials of their lives a few bones? Stoop and look into the tombs to see if you can distinguish which is the slave and which is the master, which is the poor and which is the rich. Distinguish, if such power is yours, the captive from the king, the strong from the weak, the attractive from the misshapen. So having remembered your nature you will not then be conceited.[34]

Mortality is a great equalizer. The remembrance of one's own impending death will teach the affluent humility.

Then comes Basil's exhortation to the poor, which is worth quoting at length. He encourages them with a reminder of all that God has given them in making them human. In this passage, he ascribes to them personally all the gifts and achievements that go with the divine image, which is the thing that all humans share in common.

Again, are you someone low born and obscure, a poor person born of the poor, without home or country, sick, in need every day, trembling at those in power, cowering before all because of your lowly life? Yet "one who is poor," Scripture says, "is not subjected to threats" [Prov. 13:8 LXX; my translation]. Therefore do not despair of yourself because nothing enviable belongs to you in your present circumstances, do not renounce the hope of all good; but lift up your soul toward the good things made present to you already by God, and toward the things laid up in store through his promise for later. First, then, you are a human being, the only one of the animals formed by God. Is this not enough to be reasonable grounds for the most exalted joy, that you have been entirely formed by the very hands of God [see Gen. 2:7] who has made all things? That since you have come into being according to the image of the Creator you can ascend quickly toward equality of honor with the angels through good conduct? You have been given an intellectual soul, through which

34. *Homily on the Words "Be Attentive to Yourself"* 5; trans. Harrison, *St. Basil*, 100–101.

you comprehend God, you perceive by thought the nature of beings, you pluck the sweetest fruit of wisdom.[35]

After naming the image of God, virtues, and spiritual perception, Basil speaks of preeminence over all the other animals. Then he speaks of the arts and sciences, which are possible because we are made in God's image, as we will see in chapter 8: "Further, have you not invented arts, and built cities, and devised all the things pertaining to necessity and luxury? Are not the oceans passable for you through reason? Do not earth and sea serve your life? Do not air and sky and dancing stars disclose to you their pattern?"[36]

Then Basil speaks eloquently of how the poor enjoy being surrounded by earth, sun, sky, and stars. He concludes the discussion by naming what God has done for humankind in Christ, which goes beyond the gifts of human creation:

> Now these are human things, but those of which we will now speak are still greater. These things are for your sake: God present among human beings, the distribution of the Holy Spirit, the destruction of death, the hope of resurrection, divine ordinances perfecting your life, the journey toward God through the commandments; the kingdom of heaven is ready and crowns of righteousness are prepared for one who has not fled from labors on behalf of virtue.[37]

Basil affirms the human dignity of the poor by naming many facets of the divine image. He has, in effect, summarized this book.[38] Basil encourages those tempted with discouragement and despair to remember all facets of the divine image as true

35. *Homily on the Words "Be Attentive to Yourself"* 6; trans. Harrison, *St. Basil,* 101, alt.
36. *Homily on the Words "Be Attentive to Yourself"* 6; trans. Harrison, *St. Basil,* 101.
37. *Homily on the Words "Be Attentive to Yourself"* 6; trans. Harrison, *St. Basil,* 102.
38. We will discuss related texts in the next chapter, which is about the royal dignity of those marginalized in late antique society: women, slaves, and the homeless disabled.

about themselves. Since all of these facets are God's gifts, and all people share them in common, such remembrance should foster humility as well.

The second way to acquire humility comes from the Egyptian desert. It is not easy, though it is not self-destructive as is persistently putting oneself down. Consider the following: "Again, Abba Anthony said, 'Anyone who has not been tempted cannot enter the Kingdom of Heaven.' He further added, 'Without temptation, one cannot be saved.'"[39] This saying is profoundly counterintuitive. Are not temptations, which can pressure us into committing sins, the greatest threat to our salvation? Yet if we were never tempted, if God our Father literally always answered our prayer "Lead us not into temptation," what would happen? We would slide easily into considering all our achievements and all our virtues to be the result of our own efforts or as our own possessions without any reference to God. Thus we would become separate from God instead of joining our will to his and working with him in his creative deeds. We would probably also look down on our neighbors and focus on how they lack talents, virtues, and achievements like our own. In other words, we would miss the true goals of human life.

Consider a young man who is an earnest Christian. He works very hard at practicing all the virtues we discussed earlier in this chapter. The trouble is that sooner or later he fails and falls into what he considers a disastrous sin, despite all his efforts. His hope to become a good Christian is shot down in flames. When he fell, he was probably tired in the first place from all his exertion, and so his strength was spent. He weeps and wonders what will become of him. But he has a wise and experienced spiritual adviser, so when he confesses his sin, he is reassured that God still loves him and desires his salvation.

After this happens to him over and over again, through the struggles of daily life he learns to trust God and to ask for his help and guidance in everything he does. He cannot rely on his own strength any more, because he fears another bitter failure.

39. Cited in Louf, *Way of Humility*, 30.

It is only then that he is open to receive God's continual presence, help, and guidance. Without knowing it, he has become humble. So God acts through him and begins to do wondrous things. God grants him the virtues as a gift. He accepts his situation and cooperates with God, giving God all the credit for every good action he finds himself doing. John Cassian explains what the young man experiences:

> We must ourselves learn to feel in each action both our weakness and the help of God and to proclaim daily with the saints:
> "I was pushed hard, so that I was falling,
>   but the LORD helped me.
> The LORD is my strength and my song;
> he has become my salvation." (Ps. 118:13–14 RSV)[40]

This is humility: "to feel in each action both our weakness and the help of God." Such a condition then becomes the foundation for all the virtues, for great spiritual growth, for abundant blessings to others nearby, and for the fullness of God's likeness.

---

40. *Institutes* 12.17.1; cited in Louf, *Way of Humility*, 12. Psalm translation alt.

5

Royal Dignity

We live in a society where people often hear unspoken messages that erode their awareness of possessing human dignity. Employment decisions are made on the basis of abstract mathematics that describe "the economy" instead of the concrete facts of who we are, what our family needs are, or what we can do. Government bureaucrats make decisions that affect our lives and can change those lives with one wrong keystroke on a computer. Then it takes countless hours of struggle for us to communicate with someone who can acknowledge that an error was made and fix it. Big companies want the consumer's money but have eliminated nearly all the customer service personnel that can help us over bumps in the road. Are we just interchangeable, disposable numbers on a computer screen? Not if we are made in God's image.

This chapter will address the following questions: Do I have real dignity as a human person? And does my neighbor have real dignity as a human person? The answers will provide a strong theological foundation for affirming the importance of social justice.

In the nineteenth century, a Scottish Presbyterian minister named George MacDonald became a writer of fantasy novels for children. His books are still in print and are delightful to read even today. In the early twentieth century, his young readers included J. R. R. Tolkien, who would eventually write the *Lord of the Rings*, and C. S. Lewis, who grew up to write the *Chronicles of Narnia*. They both drew inspiration from him. MacDonald imagines a reader asking him, "Why do you always write about princesses?" He replies, "Because every little girl is a princess." When the reader is confused by this answer, MacDonald asks a question in return: "What do you mean by a princess?" "The daughter of a king," replies the reader. "Very well; then every little girl is a princess," replies MacDonald.[1] Of course, he is presupposing that God is every little girl's Father.

In Genesis 1:26, God says, "Let us make the human being in our image, after our likeness; and let them have dominion over the fish of the sea, and over the birds of the air, and over the cattle, and over all the earth, and over every creeping thing that creeps upon the earth" (alt.) The word "dominion" speaks of royalty, which is a facet of the divine image in every human person. Royalty involves (1) dignity and splendor, and (2) a legitimate sovereignty rooted in one's very being. This chapter will focus on the dignity and splendor with which God has endowed every human being. The meaning of human sovereignty over the earth and its creatures will be the subject of chapter 7.

In the Roman Empire in which early Christians lived, people were generally not regarded as equal to one another but were ranked hierarchically. Men were regarded as superior to women, who were excluded from higher education and public life. There were lots of slaves, who were despised but whose labor was necessary to the economy. People with disfiguring and disabling skin diseases, known as "lepers," were excluded from their families and from society and lived as homeless beggars. Yet early Christian theologians affirmed that because women, slaves, and the

---

1. George MacDonald, *The Princess and the Goblin and The Princess and Curdie*, ed. Roderick McGillis (Oxford: Oxford University Press, 1990), 343.

homeless ill are fully human and are made in God's image, they are worthy of respect. They proclaimed that God, who judges justly, treats them better than their neighbors usually do; thus Christians should treat them better as well. Because everyone is made in the image of God, and because this image defines what it means to be human, people are fundamentally equal, regardless of the differences in wealth, education, and social status. The church preached this countercultural message in the ancient world and still preaches it now. For example, here is what Martin Luther King Jr. said in a sermon on July 4, 1965:

> The whole concept of the *imago Dei*, as it is expressed in Latin, the "image of God," is the idea that all men have something within them that God injected. Not that they have substantial unity with God, but that every man has a capacity to have fellowship with God. And this gives him a uniqueness, it gives him worth, it gives him dignity. And we must never forget this as a nation: there are no gradations in the image of God. . . . We will know one day that God made us to live together as brothers and to respect the dignity and worth of every man.[2]

In 1965 when King preached this sermon, people in our culture were not yet attentive to the problem of sexist language. If he were speaking today, surely he would say, "God made us to live together as brothers *and sisters* and to respect the dignity and worth of every *human being*." And yet today, although our culture speaks loudly about the equality of all people, in many places the message that all people are made in God's image and should be treated accordingly is still countercultural.

In this chapter, we will discuss how early Christians affirmed that women, slaves, and lepers are made in God's image. This affirmation is important, given the ways Greco-Romans, and sometimes Christians too, discriminated against these marginal-

2. Martin Luther King Jr., "The American Dream," preached at Ebenezer Baptist Church, Atlanta, Georgia, July 4, 1965, http://mlk-kpp01.stanford.edu/index.php/kingpapers/article/the_american_dream/ (accessed May 13, 2009).

ized people. Yet, significantly, despite the cultural context, some church leaders preached against such discrimination. We will see what conclusions they drew from their affirmation that all people bear God's image.

Women as God's Image

In ancient Roman society, the children of wealthy families were cared for by a slave, who took them to school, stayed in the classroom with them, then took them home again. He did not teach them to read and write, for that was their teacher's job, but he did teach them good manners and how to live an ethical life. This slave was called a "pedagogue." He was a lowly figure and people poked fun at him, but Clement of Alexandria, the second-century Christian scholar, gave the pedagogue's task real dignity when he understood it spiritually. Clement said that Christ is the true Pedagogue. Christians are like children born anew into a different way of living, so Christ guides them as they learn and practice an ethical lifestyle. Once they have learned how to live ethically, they are ready to go to class, that is, they can then learn the mysteries of God from the same Christ, who is also their Teacher.

By using the analogy of the pedagogue and the teacher, Clement explains to his upper-class audience how the spiritual journey is an educational process with different developmental stages. The desert Christians too knew that the struggle against vices and the practice of virtues come first, and the deeper kinds of prayer and insight into God's mysteries come later.

Clement uses the analogy of children to show that because both are human beings, men and women are called to make the same spiritual journey. On this journey, he says, the role of gender changes as they go through four distinct stages. The first stage is childhood, when boys and girls do the same things and are not obsessed with their differences. The second stage is adolescence and young adulthood, when couples are fascinated with their sexual differences as they court, marry, and bear children. The third stage is an older age, when husbands and wives can together devote themselves to prayer, the study of Scripture, and good works. This devotion prepares them for the final stage, the age to come, when Christian men and women face the same judgment and hope for the same reward. Clement values marriage and procreation but sees the contrast between male and female as one part in a larger process. In childhood and old age, when men and women learn from Christ and practice virtues together, they are alike as humans and prepare for their likeness to God and to each other in the next life.[3]

Clement explains that as human beings, men and women share the same virtues, which as we saw in chapter 4 is central to the image of God. They also share the same bodily experiences of food and marriage, the same senses, the same emotions, and they hope for the same rewards.

> Let us understand that the same virtue pertains to men and women. For if there is one God for both, there is also one Pedagogue for both. One church, one self-restraint, one modesty, a common food, a common marriage bond, breath, sight, hearing, knowledge, hope, obedience, love, all are alike. Those who have life in common, grace in common, and indeed salvation in common also have virtue and a way of life in common. "For in this age," Scripture says, "they marry and are given in marriage," and here alone the female and male are distinguished, "but in the age to come no longer" [see Luke 20:34–35]. There, the rewards merited by this common and holy life of marriage are reserved not for men and women but for the human being. . . . Therefore also the name "human" is common to men and women.[4]

Notice that men and women can learn the same virtues because they are coached by the same Pedagogue, Christ. The heavenly reward, Clement says, does not belong specifically to men or to women but to both, insofar as they are human. It is a full actualization of the divine likeness.

3. Clement of Alexandria, *Miscellanies* 6.100.2–3; trans. Roberts and Donaldson, ANF 2, 503; ed. Descourtieux, *Clément d'Alexandrie*, 260–62.
4. *Paedagogus* 1.4; ed. Marrou, *Clément d'Alexandrie*, 128.

This same attitude toward gender is shared by the Cappadocians and most other early Christian theologians. All of them saw examples of women, as well as men, living lives of holiness. Women could love their neighbors and offer charity as well as men could. They could also match men in the practice of ascetic disciplines. It is important to remember that these disciplines involved the bodily labor of fasting, work, and staying up at night to pray. So early Christians compared ascetics to the athletes who were much admired in Greco-Roman society, much as sports champions are today. One difference, though, is that only men were athletes, unlike today when women compete in the Olympics. Yet early Christian women could become ascetics, that is, spiritual athletes. There were desert mothers as well as fathers. Like the men, they devoted their bodies as well as their souls to the labor of prayer and the practice of virtues.

In commenting on Genesis 1:27, "God created humankind in his image, in the image of God he created them" (NRSV), Basil states that women have asked him whether they really have to carry the ethical responsibilities that belong to the image of God. In reply, Basil quotes the rest of the verse: "Male and female he created them." He concludes that women are indeed fully human, and he goes on to give examples of how they have proven it through the holiness of their lives:

> The woman also possesses creation according to the image of God, as indeed does the man. The natures are alike of equal honor, the virtues are equal, the struggles equal, the judgment alike. Let her not say, "I am weak." The weakness is in the flesh, in the soul is the power. Since indeed that which is according to God's image is of equal honor, let the virtue be of equal honor, the showing forth of good works. There is no excuse for one who wishes to allege that the body is weak. And why is it simply delicate? But through compassion it is vigorous in patient endurance and earnest in vigils. When has the nature of man been able to match the nature of woman in patiently passing through her own life? When has man been able to imitate the vigor of women in fastings, the love

of toil in prayers, the abundance in tears, the readiness for good works?[5]

Basil recognizes that the royal dignity of the human condition involves responsibilities as well as privileges and asserts that women do live up to these responsibilities. His older sister Macrina, an abbess and spiritual teacher, provided an excellent example of this. But Basil goes further. He takes care to include women's bodily strength as well, though the culture he lived in taught women that they were physically weak.

In the early church, women, like men, also accomplished that most difficult of Christian callings, martyrdom. Martyrs not only died for Christ but also suffered imprisonment in harsh conditions and torture. Like soldiers, they needed the courage and stamina to face demanding physical hardships and finally death. In fact, early Christians thought of the martyrs as Christ's soldiers. Like the athlete, the soldier was viewed as an ideal of masculinity in the Greco-Roman world. Yet just as women could be Christ's athletes through asceticism, they could also be his soldiers. This is particularly striking, because women did not serve in the armed forces, as they do in many countries today.

In a homily honoring the martyr Julitta, Basil places in her mouth a response to the implicit question, how can a weak woman face martyrdom? Julitta cites Genesis 1:27, which says that all humans are made in God's image.

"I am from the same lump [of clay]," she says, "as men. We have been made according to the image of God, as they also are. By creation, the female, with the same honor as the male, has become capable of virtue. And for what [purpose] are we of the same [human] race as men in all things? For not only flesh was taken for the fashioning of woman, but also bones from bones. So in solidity and tautness and ability to endure, we are equal to men, and this is owed by us to the Master [Christ]." Saying these things, she advanced toward the fire.[6]

5. *On the Origin of Humanity* 1.18; trans. Harrison, *St. Basil*, 45–46.
6. *Homily on the Martyr Julitta*; PG 31:240D–241A.

Here Basil depicts a dramatic scene. Julitta answers the implicit question about women by citing and interpreting Genesis. These are her last words, for she then goes willingly to be burned alive. Interestingly, she concentrates on Genesis 2:21–23, in which Eve is said to be made from Adam's rib. I remember as a child hearing misogynistic jokes in which women were called "Adam's rib" as a put down, a way of trivializing them, saying they were less or worse than men. In early Christian times, this Scripture was usually interpreted in a way opposite to the misogynistic joker's interpretation. For one thing, the word translated "rib" also means "side" in Hebrew and Greek. So in effect, the verse means that man is one "side" of humankind while woman is the other.[7] More specifically, as Julitta says, it means that woman, whom God takes from the side of man, is made of the same "stuff" as man. If humankind is like a lump of clay, woman is a piece of the same clay, broken off from the same lump that became man. Genesis 2:21–23 provided early Christians with a strong affirmation that women are fully human. This interpretation supports the statement in Genesis 1:27 that women and men are both made in the divine image.

Yet in Hebrew and Greek, the word "side" can also mean "rib." Basil's Julitta also uses this meaning to make her point. Women have bones taken from men's bones, and to her the bones represent physical strength. In the Greco-Roman world, women usually stayed indoors caring for the home, while men worked outside. So men would usually have had more exercise then women. More so than women's muscles, men's muscles would have had the solidity, tautness, and endurance that the culture valued. Julitta affirms her strength by stressing the continuity between men's bones and her own. She says that she, like a man, is capable of virtue and of serving Christ faithfully. These capacities are inherent in the human being as image of God. For Basil, her martyrdom proved her point.

7. Daniel Boyarin, *Carnal Israel: Reading Sex in Talmudic Culture* (Berkeley: University of California Press, 1993), 31–46.

Slaves as God's Image

The author of Ecclesiastes boasts, "I bought male and female slaves" (2:7). In a homily on this text, Gregory of Nyssa uses the statement in Genesis 1 that human beings bear the divine image to scold owners for keeping slaves. In a society where slavery was taken for granted as an intrinsic part of the economy and was supported by the legal system, Gregory provides a vigorous theological critique of the whole idea of slavery. In its passion for social justice, his writing has direct relevance today. As we saw in chapter 1, Gregory emphasizes human freedom as being central to the divine image. He again emphasizes freedom in this passage, together with royal dignity:

> "I bought male and female slaves." What are you saying? You condemn to slavery the human being, whose nature is free and self-ruling, and you legislate in opposition to God, overturning what is according to the law of nature. For upon the one who was created to be lord of the earth and appointed to rule the creation, upon this one you impose the yoke of slavery. . . . You have forgotten the limits of your authority, a rule limited to dominion over the nonrational animals. For scripture says, "Let them rule birds and fish and quadrupeds and reptiles" [see Gen. 1:26]. How can you bypass the slavery within your power and rise up against the one who is free by nature, numbering one of the same nature as yourself among the four-legged and legless beasts?[8]

Here, in his *Fourth Homily on Ecclesiastes*, Gregory stresses that human beings possess in this life the divine image, with all the dignity, equality, and authority that belong to it. This includes slaves, the people most subject to the miseries caused by the fallenness of society.

Citing Genesis 1:26, he notes that God made animals, and not their fellow human beings, subject to human authority. Nyssa, where Gregory served as a pastor, was a small town. Many of his parishioners must have been farmers and would have understood

---

8. *Fourth Homily on Ecclesiastes*; GNO 5:335.

their "rule" of animals from their daily experience. They rode horses and had oxen pull their plows. They lived with animals every day, took care of them, and worked alongside them to grow the food they needed to live. We will say more about the relationship of humans and the natural world—an issue of great urgency today—in chapter 7.

In this homily, Gregory goes on to say that this ultimate form of class difference, namely, that between owners and slaves, splits the unity that properly belongs to humankind. Again he speaks directly to the slaveholder:

> You have divided [human] nature itself, making some live as slaves and others as lords. . . . For God said, "Let us make a human being according to our image and likeness" [Gen. 1:26, my translation]. Who sells and who buys the one who is in the likeness of God and rules all the earth and all that is on the earth, having been assigned the authority by God?[9]

In the Greco-Roman world, when a slave was sold all his property was sold with him. So Gregory goes on to say that the prospective slave owns and rules the earth and everything in it and is himself of greater value than all he owns, so no imaginable price could be sufficient to buy him. Then Gregory cites Matthew 16:26 and says, "For he who knows human nature," that is, Jesus, "says precisely that the whole world is not of sufficient value to be exchanged for the soul of a human being."[10]

Gregory goes on to tell the master what he has in common with his slave. His list parallels the list of human characteristics that Clement of Alexandria says men and women have in common (cited above) and the list that Basil says the poor possess because they are human (cited at the end of chapter 4, above):

> For what has the authority [of ownership] added to what is yours by nature? Not time, not beauty, not honor, not furtherance in

9. *Fourth Homily on Ecclesiastes*; GNO 5:336.
10. *Fourth Homily on Ecclesiastes*; GNO 5:337.

virtue. He is made of the same stuff as you, his life is of a like kind; you who are lord and the one subjected to lordship are to an equal extent dominated by the passions of soul and body: pain and good cheer, joy and sadness, grief and pleasure, anger and fear, sickness and death. Is there any difference in these matters between the slave and the lord? Do they not breathe the same air? Do they not alike see the sun? Do they not alike preserve their nature by eating food? Are they not the same in their use of digestive organs? Are not the two one dust after death? Is the judgment not one? Do they not share a common kingdom and a common hell? How then can you who have equality in everything have superiority in any particular, as you say, supposing yourself as a human being to be master of a human being?[11]

Early Christians like Clement, Basil, and Gregory were always attentive to what human beings have in common, insofar as they are human. The shared experiences of humans make them truly neighbors. Moreover, their capacity to be in relationship with God is their most important common feature. When Christians look at the human experience from God's perspective, the differences between men and women, or owners and slaves, look small compared to issues all people face, such as divine judgment and salvation.

Lepers as God's Image

In the Greco-Roman world, there was a great fear of leprosy. People knew it was contagious, so they wanted to avoid anyone thought to have it for fear of catching it themselves. So those who had leprosy or any skin disease that looked as though it might be leprosy were excluded from the community. They were driven away by their families and excluded from houses in town. They lost their relatives, their social status, their jobs, and their livelihoods. So they lived in groups in the open fields, destitute, and cared for each other. They ran from other people, warning that they were "unclean." And yet they had to beg from

11. *Fourth Homily on Ecclesiastes*; GNO 5:338.

others for food in order to survive. Having destroyed eyes and limbs one by one, leaving the leper disabled and disfigured, the leprosy killed them. AIDS is the closest contemporary analogy to this dreaded disease and the stigma attached to it, but more broadly speaking, all who are disabled and homeless share the ancient leper's lot.

Basil built a home and hospital for lepers just outside his city of Caesarea. It was a big charitable project. His eloquent friend Gregory of Nazianzus made a fundraising tour in which he preached a powerful sermon about how Christians must help the poor, especially lepers. Basil's brother Gregory of Nyssa must have helped too. In his sermon *On Love of the Poor*, Gregory of Nyssa describes the miserable condition of lepers before making the point that the leper is made in God's image:

> He is a human being, created according to the image of God, appointed to rule the earth, having within his power the service of the nonrational animals. In this misfortune he has indeed been changed to such an extent that from his appearance it is doubtful whether his visible form with the identifying marks it bears is clearly that of a human being or of some other animal.[12]

For Gregory of Nyssa, it is scandalous for the slave to have to play the role of a nonrational animal, such as a working animal on a farm. Similarly, he considers it an outrage that illness and mistreatment have blurred the distinction between a leprous human being and a beast. In both cases, one bearing the divine image is denied the respect intended by God. Divisions of class and social status have broken the unity and solidarity intrinsic to the human condition shared by owners and slaves and by those secure in their houses and those wandering homeless in the countryside.

In his fundraising sermon, Gregory of Nazianzus speaks at length about lepers and about poverty in general. Like the other early Christians quoted in this chapter, he lists the things lepers share with all other human persons. He calls them "our brothers

12. *On Love of the Poor*; ed. Heck, *Gregorii Nysseni*, 26.

and sisters before God . . . who share the same nature with us, who have been put together from the same clay from which we first came." Like all of us they are embodied; they have nerves and bones, flesh and skin. Yet for Gregory the moral and spiritual things all people share in common are most important.

> If I must speak of greater things, [lepers] have been made in the image of God in the same way you and I have, and perhaps preserve that image better than we, even if their bodies are corrupted. They have put on the same Christ in the inner person [see Eph. 3:16–17], and have been entrusted with the same pledge of the Spirit [see 2 Cor. 1:22]. They share in the same laws as we do, the same Scriptural teachings, the same covenants and liturgical gatherings, the same sacraments, the same hopes. Christ died for them as he did for us, taking away the sin of the whole world [see John 1:29]; they are heirs with us of the life to come [see 1 Cor. 8:17], even if they have missed out on a great deal of life here on earth. They have been buried together with Christ, and have risen with him [see Rom. 6:4; Col. 2:12]. If they suffer with him, it is so that they may share in his glory [see Rom. 8:17].[13]

For Gregory, to be made in the image of God is to have the capacity to receive salvation in its fullness. To preserve the image is to make choices in life that lead toward this salvation. The lepers shared with all people the hope of a life together with Christ in the age to come. A leper had to endure many sufferings patiently and rely on God's help to get through each day. In fact, Gregory says, he may be preserving the divine likeness, the imprint of royalty, better than Gregory's prosperous audience is.

Gregory concludes his long, impassioned appeal for financial support by citing Matthew 25:31–46, in which Christ identifies the needy with himself:

> If you believe me at all, then, servants and brothers and sisters and fellow heirs of Christ, let us take care of Christ while there

13. *Oration* 14.14; trans. Daley, *Gregory of Nazianzus*, 83, alt.

is still time. Let us minister to Christ's needs, let us give Christ nourishment, let us clothe Christ, let us gather Christ in, let us show Christ honor, . . . not just with gold and frankincense and myrrh, like the Magi. . . . Let us give this gift to him through the needy, who today are cast down on the ground, so that when we all are released from this place, they may receive us into the eternal tabernacle, in Christ himself, who is our Lord, to whom be glory for all the ages. Amen.[14]

Notice that the donors are also united with Christ. They share his royal dignity and are members of his family. This makes lepers, slaves, and all the needy their family members, because the poor have been made members of Christ's family. People's dignity, their relationship with Christ, is what enables them to help others as well as to receive help. The family connection, which Christ establishes, brings them together and enables the gifts to reach the places where they are most needed.

Affirming Royal Dignity Today

Children in royal families are trained to serve their country throughout their lives. They learn to be gracious to everyone they meet, to pay attention to who others are and what their life experiences have been, and to think of what to say that will put the other at ease. This kind of behavior is what George MacDonald has in mind when he speaks of a little girl being a princess.[15] His hope is that every little girl can learn these skills, and every little boy too. Being made in God's image, and thus being endowed with royalty, is what enables people to value and care for others.

In the world today there are indeed many people in need of care. People suffer discrimination because of race, class, gender, nationality, and disability, among other things. Moreover, though the practice is illegal just about everywhere and is therefore hidden, there are many slaves in today's world who are at the bottom

14. *Oration* 14.40; trans. Daley, *Gregory of Nazianzus*, 97.
15. See the character of young Princess Irene in *The Princess and the Goblin*.

of the social ladder and live in some of the worst conditions. These are people who have been forced or tricked into working with no pay and are held captive so that they cannot escape. Gregory of Nyssa said that a slave, a human being made in God's image, is worth more than the whole physical world and asks what price can ever be enough to buy one. He would be shocked to learn how much the price has fallen. Kevin Bales, an expert on contemporary slavery, says that it has existed throughout history but that today there is one major difference:

> The one part of slavery that is new is the complete collapse in the price of slaves. For most of human history slaves were expensive, the average cost being around $40,000 in today's money. That price has now fallen to an all-time historical low. The average slave costs around $90 today. This dramatic change in the economic equation of slavery means that slaves have stopped being capital purchase items and are now disposable inputs in economic processes.[16]

In the late antique Mediterranean world of the early Christians, or in pre–Civil War America, owners had an economic incentive to take care of their slaves to avoid losing their investment. They provided stable housing, food, and sometimes health care. Today, by contrast, a slave who becomes sick or refuses to be cooperative may be killed or simply put out on the street with no resources to survive, no job skills, and no contacts.

E. Benjamin Skinner, a courageous journalist, travelled to several countries—Haiti, Sudan, Rumania, and India—to find slaves, slaveholders, and slave brokers and tell their stories to the world.[17] He shows how slaves are brutalized and made to

16. See www.freetheslaves.net/NETCOMMUNITY/Page.aspx?pid=304&srcid= 183 (accessed June 23, 2008). This is the website of Bales's advocacy organization, Free the Slaves, and it contains much information about contemporary slavery. For a detailed discussion of slavery today, and the human consequences of the drop in price, see Kevin Bales, *Disposable People: New Slavery in the Global Economy*, 2nd ed. (Berkeley: University of California Press, 2004).

17. The result is his book *A Crime So Monstrous: Face-to-Face with Modern-Day Slavery* (New York: Free Press, 2008).

work long hours under threat of violence so that they lose the sense of their own identity and human dignity. For centuries in Haiti, a desperately poor nation with a largely ineffective government, there have been child slaves called *restavèks*. This Creole word comes from the French words for "stay with" and refers to children who live with families who are not their own. These children work from before dawn until bedtime every day caring for their masters' homes and children.

Skinner recounts the story of Bill Nathan, a *restavèk* who was finally rescued and went on to have a good life, a rare outcome for those with childhoods like his. Shortly after Bill was born in 1984, his father died of malaria. Without his income, Bill's mother had to support him and his sister. She went to a small town to look for work and met an American nun, Sister Catherine, who helped her find a home. She worked doing laundry and cooking for wealthier neighbors and lovingly cared for her two children with what little money she had. Sister Catherine arranged for Bill to go to school. In 1991, when he was seven years old, his mother suddenly became ill and died. She had arranged that in case she died, her two employers would care for Bill and his sister. So each child went to one of the employers. They were now orphans, and, without their mother intending it, they became *restavèks*, child slaves. Bill never saw his sister again.

Bill soon had to quit school, and he worked long hours. When he worked too slowly or made a mistake, he was beaten. Once he was given money and asked to shop at the market for the family, but told to do so quickly. He ran all the way into town, and when he got there, exhausted, he was tricked into betting the money on a shell game and lost it all. His mistress found out about it from others before he got home.

"You bet the money!" [she] screamed, "And you know we don't have any money in the house!"
Bill tried to speak but choked on tears instead. She kicked him to his knees. Then she handed him two rocks, one in either hand, and told him to hold his arms extended, and not to drop the rocks or she would kill him.

The martinet [a whip] first fell on his back. He held his tongue, and held on to his rocks. Then she beat him harder. As Bill screamed, she whipped him everywhere—his head, even his eyes. The other children watched in horror. After twenty minutes, Bill's blood lay in pools on the cement floor. The rocks were still in his hands.[18]

In 1994, Bill "entered his eleventh year of life, and his third year of what slavery scholar Orlando Patterson terms 'social death.'" Haitians have another term for *restavèks* who have absorbed their slave status: "zombified."[19] As if he had no will of his own, he did the will of his masters. His memory of freedom faded, and so did his will to escape.

Then one day, two men came to the door and took him away. They had been sent by Sr. Catherine, and they took him to her convent. She had heard about his beatings and knew his mother would never have approved of his treatment. She fed and bathed him and gave him sandals. Then she sent him to an orphanage in Port-au-Prince. He was happy there. The man who ran the orphanage discovered that Bill had a talent for drumming and arranged to have him sent to Gambia to study percussion. Bill Nathan became a drummer in a band, and in 2002 they were touring and playing internationally. At their concerts he would tell his story and speak out about slavery in Haiti. He had grown into a strong and gentle man with faith in God, and he now works to free other slaves.[20]

Slaveholders not only mistreat slaves but work to eradicate their awareness of the dignity and identity that go with being human. Like Sr. Catherine, Christians—and human beings generally—have a responsibility to look for ways to help free them. Indeed, there are many tasks that belong to those made in the divine image. Fighting global slavery is some people's vocation, but others are given other vocations. Women, the disabled, the homeless, the poor, and all the marginalized also need atten-

18. Skinner, *Crime So Monstrous*, 22–23.
19. Skinner, *Crime So Monstrous*, 38.
20. Bill's story is told in Skinner, *Crime So Monstrous*, 18–23, 38–41.

tion and care. We can each find a task that corresponds to our gifts and glorifies God while serving our neighbors or caring for the created world. Yet it is our responsibility to find ways to affirm the full humanity—the royal dignity—of all people, especially those we meet each day, and of those whom others are inclined to despise.

6

Embodiment

The monks of Egypt worked with their hands. At harvest time some of them would work temporarily for farmers, helping to pick the fruits and vegetables and thereby earning wages they could use throughout the year. Some of them cared for the sick, but almost all offered hospitality to each other or to pilgrims who came from far away to see them. So with their hands they brought in the harvest, nursed patients, or cooked and served meals. Some grew their own vegetable gardens. But most often they gathered the palm leaves that were so plentiful in Egypt. They took the leaves to their cells and stored them, letting them dry. Then they moistened a few at a time to make them pliable and wove them into baskets, mats, ropes, or fishing nets. The monks would then sell the products of their cottage industry, and these products served the buyers' daily needs.

The monks used their profits to meet their needs for food and other simple things and gave any remaining money to the poor. Abba Poemen told a brother, "As far as you can, do some manual work so as to be able to give alms, for it is written that alms and faith purify from sin."[1] That is, not one or the other by itself but both alms and faith, both the body's work and the mind's work, purify one from sin.

The work the early monks and nuns did with their hands was also an integral part of their spiritual practice. For all who followed him to the desert, Abba Anthony set an example of combining manual labor with prayer. His followers preserved a story of how an angel taught him this practice. They placed it first in the Greek collection of desert stories, which shows that they considered it to be foundational. It explains how an essential monastic rhythm of life came to be. "When the holy Abba Anthony lived in the desert he was beset by listlessness, and attacked by many sinful thoughts." Listlessness, or restless boredom, was a powerful temptation in a desert cell. The result of this passion is that a monk does not feel like doing any of the disciplines he is committed to doing and wishes he were somewhere else. This wish is accompanied by depression and followed by all kinds of other sinful thoughts. Then the mind cannot focus on prayer. The body also becomes restless. When Anthony found himself in this condition, he felt desperate. He prayed for help and guidance:

> He said to God, "Lord, I want to be saved but these thoughts do not leave me alone; what shall I do in my affliction? How can I be saved?" A short while afterwards, when he got up to go out, Anthony saw a man like himself sitting at his work, getting up from his work to pray, then sitting down and plaiting a rope, then getting up again to pray. It was an angel of the Lord sent to correct and reassure him, "Do this, and you will be saved." At these words, Anthony was filled with joy and courage. He did this, and he was saved.[2]

He alternated between prayer and manual labor, and this alternation became a rhythm throughout the day. It enabled him to maintain a balance so he could turn his attention first to one, then to the other.

1. Poemen 69; trans. Ward, *Sayings*, 176.
2. Anthony 1; trans. Ward, *Sayings*, 1–2, alt.

So Anthony had to plait palm leaves in order to stay focused on prayer. This means that his body was essential to his spiritual practice. To be sure, he needed his hands at work to love and serve his neighbors, but he also needed them in order to pray. Desert asceticism aimed to restore the whole human being to balance and wholeness. Since body and mind are intimately connected—as scientists in our own time know very well—both must work together to seek God. Poemen says that a monk's life in his cell involves manual work and fasting as well as silence and prayer.[3] The desert monks and nuns prayed by standing on their feet, speaking aloud with their mouths, holding their hands outstretched so that their whole body imitated the form of a cross, and staying awake at night. What they did with their bodies cleared their minds so they were able to focus their thoughts on God. Taking breaks for prayer also helped them focus on their work.

Some communities of monks believed that they should pray all the time and not do any work. This position was rejected by the early church and by more mainstream monks. The controversy over this issue may be one reason why Anthony's story about the angel was considered so important. The dispute probably arose because monks were supposed to be like angels, who are spirits without bodies. So some of them were tempted to disregard the body or to try to get away from its needs. Yet they learned from experience that ignoring the body's genuine needs is self-defeating.

This point is illustrated by another desert story. As was often done in the Egyptian desert, a younger monk lived with an older one, who set an example for him and served as his mentor:

> It was said of Abba John the Short, that one day he said to his older brother, "I would like to be free of all care, like the angels, who do not work, but ceaselessly offer worship to God." So he took off his cloak and went away into the desert. After a week he came back to his brother. When he knocked on the door, he heard his brother say, before he opened it, "Who are you?"

3. Poemen 168; trans. Ward, *Sayings*, 190.

He said, "I am John, your brother." But he replied, "John has become an angel, and henceforth he is no longer among men." The other begged him, saying, "It is I." However, his brother did not let him in, but left him there in distress until morning. Then, opening the door, he said to him, "You are a man and must once again work in order to eat." Then John made a prostration before him, saying, "Forgive me."[4]

Thus John learned that he had to include his body and its needs in his disciplined life.

The monks learned from experience that they needed their bodies to live a spiritual life. So they had to take care of them. The body was, and today still is, an indispensable partner to the soul and mind in the work of serving one's neighbors and of prayer to God. Through experimentation with different lifestyles and practices, early monks and nuns discovered the answer to a perennial human question, "How is my body important to who I am?"

Yet early Christians also found that at times the body gets in the way of prayer. However intense one's spiritual experience, one has to stop praying, after all, in order to eat or to sleep. Bodily needs demand attention. Gregory of Nazianzus reflected on the limitations caused by embodiment in his sermon on the homeless disabled.[5] The lepers' example may have led him to think of his own struggles with illness. He expresses ambivalence, calling his body "a cordial enemy and a treacherous friend."[6] And yet he acknowledges forthrightly his body's value in working with him toward his salvation: "I have no other helper to use in striving for what is best, since I know what I was made for, and know that I must ascend towards God through my actions."[7] He knows he was made for virtuous deeds and that virtues are forms of likeness to God. The body together with

4. John the Dwarf 2; trans. Ward, *Sayings*, 86, alt. I have adopted an alternative version of the monk's name, John the Short, from Ward's more recent translation of the Latin sayings collection.

5. See chapter 5.

6. *Oration* 14.7; trans. Daley, *Gregory of Nazianzus*, 79.

7. *Oration* 14.6; trans. Daley, *Gregory of Nazianzus*, 79.

the soul and mind, therefore, can make essential contributions to the human person's divine likeness.

Soul and Body

Early Christians were certain that the human mind is made in God's image. The intellect, the highest part of the soul according to Plato and other philosophers, is the part of us that fulfills several central activities of the image and likeness of God. It exercises free choice; it perceives spiritual realities, such as God, angels, and other human minds; it acts virtuously and leads the other parts of the human person in virtuous actions. Yet the body also actually *does* virtuous actions. So how do body and soul work together? In other words, how is my body important to who I am?

Basil and Gregory of Nyssa speak of how skillfully God designed and made the human body to house the soul. It is constructed to encourage and enable the activities of the divine image. Basil explains how the difference in bodily posture between a human being and a sheep corresponds to their differing activities and purposes. He addresses his congregation:

> God created you upright. He gave this special structure to you as distinct from the rest of the animals.
> Why?
> Because the activity he intended to give you is also special. For they are grazing animals, and they are structured in accord with the things toward which they aim by nature. The sheep was created to go to pasture. It has its head inclining downward, looking at the stomach and the parts below the stomach, since the fulfillment of happiness for these animals is filling the stomach and enjoying pleasure. Yet the human being no longer looks toward the stomach, but his head is lifted high toward things above, that he may look up to what is akin to him.[8]

Basil adds that the "things above" are Christ and the heavenly realities, toward which humans are created to turn their

---

8. *On the Origin of Humanity* 2.15; trans. Harrison, *St. Basil*, 61, alt.

attention and their desire. The sheep's head bows toward the earth and points back toward its stomach and further back toward its organs of procreation. These body parts represent its preoccupations: food and reproduction. Basil exhorts his listeners to look up toward God instead. This example shows how Basil sees the structure of the human body as fashioned to support the fulfillment of the proper aims of the image of God, namely, to know God in Christ and become united with him.

Gregory of Nyssa goes much further than his brother in analyzing how the body's structure fits the activities of the image of God. Basil says that standing upright is important because it places the head and the eyes at the top so they can look upward toward the heavens. Gregory says the upright posture frees the hands so they do not have to serve as feet. The hands, therefore, can be guided by reason to do all kinds of tasks, including writing.[9] Human cultures are made possible by the great variety of tasks that the mind can invent and the hands can do, such as the arts, the sciences, and manufacturing. Writing also builds complex interpersonal communication and elaborate social structures, and it enables the preservation of memories and culture from generation to generation. Gregory adds that because people, unlike nonrational animals, use their hands to acquire food, their mouths, lips, tongues, and teeth are no longer needed for that purpose and have been shaped as organs of speech, which again serves reason and interpersonal communication.[10]

Speech, writing, and creative work are ways for our souls and minds to communicate with the world around us, including other people.[11] The organs of speech and the hands are thus vital links between the soul, which is spiritual, and the world that allow us to touch not only spiritual but also material realities. These bodily organs enable us to commu-

9. On the Creation of Humanity 8.1–2; trans. Moore and Wilson, Gregory, 393.

10. On the Creation of Humanity 8.8; trans. Moore and Wilson, Gregory, 394–95.

11. On the Creation of Humanity 9.1; trans. Moore and Wilson, Gregory, 395.

nicate something of ourselves to earthly creatures and to the biosphere as a whole. Through the medium of the material world, through speech, writing, and culture, they also reach out to other human beings, who are made in God's image, and form communities. Thus the body plays an essential part in the vocations of the divine image in the natural world, in human culture, and in human community. These three vocations are the subjects, respectively, of the next three chapters of this book.

So mouth and hands are the means of communication from the human mind to the world. How, according to Gregory of Nyssa, are realities in the world communicated to the mind? The answer is through the senses: sight, hearing, smell, and so on. Thus the sensory organs—eyes, ears, nose, and the like—play an essential role. The mind receives inputs from the various senses and organizes them into one, coherent perception. For instance, I can see a cantaloupe's tan and orange colors, feel its weight and rough surface, and smell its aroma; yet I know that these sensations come from one fruit. Mind also provides memory, where the various sensory perceptions are archived.[12] So I remember last summer's cantaloupe. Once I perceive and remember the world around me, I can think of how best to respond. The physical senses, then, are the mediators between the material world and the mind. Together with hands and speech organs, and thus the whole body, they enable us to function as God's image and likeness.

The Body and the Fall

At the beginning of his book *On the Creation of Humanity*, Gregory of Nyssa explains what God intends the royal human creature to do. God has created the world as a beautiful palace filled with treasures, that is, the plants and animals, and then makes the sovereign, that is, the human person, and introduces him to the environment. Thus God "manifests [the human being]

---

12. *On the Creation of Humanity* 10; trans. Moore and Wilson, *Gregory*, 395–96.

in the world to behold some of the wonders in it and be the lord of others. So by his enjoyment he may have knowledge of the Giver, and, by the beauty and majesty of the things he has seen he may trace the power of the Maker, which is beyond speech and language."[13] In other words, the human is to use his or her eyes, to look around the natural world, and to delight in its beauty. All this would lead to knowledge of God and God's marvelous creativity.

Gregory goes on to explain the purpose of the human person's twofold powers of perception, that is, the soul's ability to perceive spiritual realities and the bodily senses' ability to perceive the natural world. Originally these two kinds of perception supported each other and together enabled the human to delight in the Creator. The human person is composed of realities derived from God and from the created world, that is, from the divine image and from the earth. So his or her very identity links him or her with both God and the natural world, and this linkage is at the root of our powers of perception: God blends "the divine and the earthly, so that by means of both [the human person] may have kinship and closeness to each enjoyment. Thus he enjoys God through his more divine nature, and the good things of earth through the sense perception that is akin to them."[14] So for Gregory, the body and the senses are good. They are essential to fulfilling our purpose of looking with love toward God. In fact, the earth and its creatures are themselves good and unspeakably beautiful, and by looking toward them one can see the Creator in his work.

In these texts, Gregory has described how things occurred in paradise according to God's plan. It is essential to remember this picture when considering Gregory's description of the fall and sin later in the same book. He begins by describing the human mind's close relationship with God, a topic we discussed in chapter 3:

13. On the Creation of Humanity 2.1; trans. Moore and Wilson, Gregory, 390, alt.
14. On the Creation of Humanity 2.2; trans. Moore and Wilson, Gregory, 390, alt.

All things that have a desire for what is beautiful and good incline toward the most beautiful and supreme good of all, that is, the divinity itself. Therefore, we say that since the mind is in the image of the most beautiful, it also remains in beauty and goodness as long as it participates as far as possible in its likeness to the archetype. But if it were at all to depart from this [likeness], it would be stripped of the beauty in which it had been.[15]

Gregory of Nyssa thus has essentially the same understanding of the fall that we saw in Athanasius, though he analyzes it differently. The fall is caused by the human person's choice to turn away from God, who is the source of life, as Athanasius says, and, as Gregory emphasizes, the source of goodness and beauty. Since the mind is the image of God, it derives its beauty from its model, God, through participation. Yet this participation requires an active choice to continue looking toward God, desiring his life and his likeness, and opening oneself to receive what one desires.

Gregory uses the metaphor of a mirror to name this receptivity. The mind's mirror receives light into itself from the divine source and receives the likeness of that source. The light that travels from the source to the mirror establishes a contact, a genuine sharing, between God and the human mind:

And, as we have said, the mind is adorned by the likeness of the archetypal beauty, being formed as though it were a mirror to receive the imprint of that which it displays. We consider that the nature governed by it [that is, the body] has the same relation to the mind. That nature is itself adorned by the mind's beauty and becomes, as it were, a mirror of the mirror.[16]

Gregory affirms that the human mind, bearing God's image, mediates between God and the person's own body. The body

15. *On the Creation of Humanity* 12.9; trans. Moore and Wilson, *Gregory*, 398–99, alt. Recall that Gregory does not distinguish between the divine image and the divine likeness in the human person.

16. *On the Creation of Humanity* 12.9; trans. Moore and Wilson, *Gregory*, 399, alt.

too is like a mirror, capable of receiving the divine light. Yet the
mind must choose to receive that light from the divine source
and then pass it along to the body. The body, then, is "a mirror
of the mirror," that is, an image of the image of God.

So if everything goes as God has planned, the body will share
the divine image with its soul. Matter will then receive and
share the beauty of God, more than it does now. To be sure,
everything in the world manifests God's presence and beauty
because God is present in it as its Creator. Yet the divine image
possesses a greater share in God's presence and in the divine
light and beauty that God himself has imprinted into the human
person. So we have the task of sharing this divine light first with
our own bodies and then through our bodies with the world
around us so that it all becomes like the bush Moses saw that
burned with divine glory but was not itself consumed (see Exod.
3:2–3). We will discuss this process further in the next chapter,
but now we need to understand how Gregory thought the fall
interrupted it.

For Gregory, the mind, and not the body, is responsible for
the fall. The mind turns its attention away from God toward
material things, namely, the body and the earth. Then, to use
Gregory's metaphor, the mirror turns its back on God so the
light from God hits only the back of the mirror, not its receptive,
reflective front surface. The sequence of communication is then
interrupted. The light never reaches the mind. Since the mind
is unillumined, light never moves from mind to body either.
The body, like all of God's creation, manifests the Creator's
glory, but not in the same way or to the same extent as if it
received divine light through the human mind. However, once
the mind is cut off from God, it can no longer see God's glory
in material things. Nor does the mind that has turned away
from God have in itself the beauty of the divine image. Then,
sadly, the original process works in reverse. Lack of beauty is
conveyed to the mind as it gazes toward matter, apart from
God, who is the source of beauty. In mind and soul the human
person has forgotten God and is immersed in a material world
with no awareness of God's presence, much like many people

in the world today. This is the fallen condition. It turns God's creative plan upside down.[17]

Yet it is important to note that for Gregory, looking toward matter is not itself sinful. Adam and Eve in paradise had the task of mediating between God and the material world. As we saw above, they were supposed to look toward matter, see God's beauty in it, and praise God for it. So they were supposed to hold an awareness of both God and the created world at the same time. This activity is part of the royal priestly ministry we will discuss in the next chapter; it is an essential facet of the divine image. The sin of the first humans was to turn away from God, turning their backs to him instead of their mirrors.

Christ Redeems the Body

In Jesus Christ, God heals the damage caused by the fall. After all, Christians believe that Christ assumed flesh and lived a human, bodily life, thereby uniting his flesh with God and using it to do divine works. He accomplished salvation by suffering in the flesh on the cross. As a result, his body was raised from the dead. So like Paul, Christians hope for their own resurrection, and this hope encompasses the whole creation as well:

> For the creation waits with eager longing for the revealing of the children of God; . . . in hope that the creation itself will be set free from its bondage to decay and will obtain the freedom of the glory of the children of God. We know that the whole creation has been groaning in labor pains until now; and not only the creation, but we ourselves, who have the first fruits of the Spirit, groan inwardly while we wait for adoption, the redemption of our bodies. (Rom. 8:19–23 NRSV)

After Paul, the second-century theologian Irenaeus is perhaps the clearest of the early Christian writers in his affirmation of the positive role the flesh plays in the process of redemption.

---

17. *On the Creation of Humanity* 12.10–12; trans. Moore and Wilson, *Gregory*, 399.

Through his incarnation, Christ extends his reign from heaven to earth, and through his death he extends it to the realm of the dead. He comes to all the places that have been alienated from God by the fall in order to reveal God there in and through his flesh. Then human beings, who have lost contact with their spiritual perception, are able to see him through their bodily senses. Irenaeus explains the result of Christ's coming:

> As he reigned in heaven so the Word of God reigns on earth . . . and holds sway, too, over the things which are under the earth, having become "the first-born from the dead" [Col. 1:18 RSV], so that, as we have said, all things might behold their King, so that the fatherly light might meet and rest upon the flesh of our Lord, and then, from that resplendent flesh, come upon us, and finally so that the human, girded with the fatherly light, might attain to incorruption.[18]

The divine light comes ultimately from God the Father and is fully present in the Son. So when the Son becomes incarnate as Jesus Christ, Irenaeus says, we can know him and thus receive him because this same light shines forth from his flesh. It comes easily from there to us, since we are also embodied. The result is that in Christ we are clothed in the divine light, which will bring us incorruption, that is, freedom from decay and from death. We saw how Gregory of Nyssa describes the fall as breaking the link by which light reaches from God through the human mind and body to the created world. In this text, Irenaeus shows how Christ, through the incarnation, has restored the connection between the divine light and his body. From there it radiates to our bodies and, ultimately, to the whole created world, as Paul says in Romans 8.

Elsewhere Irenaeus speaks again of how Christ's embodiment reveals God to humankind:

> There was no other way by which we could learn the things of God than for our Teacher, who is the Word, to become man. No

---

18. *Against Heresies* 4.20.2; trans. Saward, *Scandal of the Incarnation*, 52, alt.

other could have revealed to us the secrets of the Father, none but the Father's very own Word. "For who [else] has known the mind of the Lord, or who has been his counselor?" [Rom. 11:34 RSV]. Again, there was no other way for us to learn than to see our Teacher and hear his voice with our own ears. It is by becoming imitators of his actions and doers of his words that we have communion with him. It is from him who has been perfect from before all creation that we, so lately made, receive fulfillment.[19]

So we learn of God through our ears. By learning from Christ's example and his teachings, we can know how to do God's will. And when we choose to do it, which for Irenaeus is an essential step in growing toward salvation, then we have communion with God. And through this communion, or in other words, from him, we receive our perfection and our fulfillment.

In another place, Irenaeus uses Paul's metaphor of the olive tree being grafted (Rom. 11:17–24) to explain the human condition. A cultivated olive that is neglected, he says, will in time grow the same kind of inedible fruit as the wild olive. This is our fallen condition, yet God can reverse the process so that the tree is cultivated again and grows good fruit.

[The wild olive trees] can, if they are carefully tended and accept the grafting of the Word [see James 1:21], return to the pristine human nature, the nature, that is, which was created in the image and likeness of God. Just as a grafted wild olive does not lose the substance of its wood, but changes the quality of its fruit . . . so the human, when he [or she] is grafted in by faith and receives the Spirit of God, does not lose the substance of flesh, but changes the quality of those fruits which are his [or her] works.[20]

In other words, the composition of our bodies, like the wood, remains the same whether we are in paradise, are fallen, or are redeemed. Again, material flesh is not the cause of the fall. What

19. *Against Heresies* 5.1.1; trans. Saward, *Scandal of the Incarnation*, 57.
20. *Against Heresies* 5.10.2; trans. Saward, *Scandal of the Incarnation*, 106, alt.

changes is the way the human person functions as a whole—how we live and what we do—and thus the fruits of our lives. The character of our lives can change radically, and so can the results of our actions and the impact of our lives on the people and the world around us. And yet we still have the same bodies.

The Joy of Service

Gregory of Nazianzus, the friend and colleague of Gregory of Nyssa, says that an important task of the mind or soul is to educate the body. In Platonic fashion, he thinks of the soul as the higher part of ourselves and the body as the lower part, but, as he explains, the soul's fulfillment of its task will transform this hierarchical relationship. It is the soul's responsibility to "draw to itself and raise up that which is lower, by gradually releasing it from its heaviness, so that what God is to the soul, the soul may become to the body, itself educating the matter that serves it, and bringing it, as its fellow servant, near to God."[21] At the start, God, soul, and body have the same kind of relationship that Gregory of Nyssa described in terms of mirrors. Here, for Gregory of Nazianzus, the soul serves God and the body serves the soul. So instead of light shining down, authority and direction extend from God through the soul to the body. The body's "heaviness," which is a result of the fall, causes it to resist moving upward with the soul toward God. Yet the soul, guided by God, is called to educate the body in a way that will transform its relationship to the body. Despite any heaviness, the soul can draw the body upward and teach it to be a fellow servant, or a colleague, in service to God. Then body and soul are united harmoniously and collaborate in following God's direction. Side by side, they share the hope of receiving a heavenly reward for their faithful service.

As we saw earlier, desert fathers like John the Short also learned that soul and body have to work together. Young John

21. *Oration* 2.17; ed. Bernardi, *Grégoire de Nazianze*, 112.

learned the lesson of bodily service well, as we see in the following story:

> Some old men were entertaining themselves at Scetis [a large monastic settlement in Egypt] by having a meal together; among them was Abba John. A venerable priest got up to offer drink, but nobody accepted any from him, except John the Short. They were surprised and said to him, "How is it that you, the youngest, dared to let yourself be served by the priest?" Then he said to them, "When I get up to offer drink, I am glad when everyone accepts it, since I am receiving my reward; that is the reason, then, that I accepted it, so that he also might gain his reward and not be grieved by seeing that no one would accept anything from him." When they heard this, they were all filled with wonder and edification at his discretion.[22]

Remember how John tried to go off by himself to praise God like an angel? His empty stomach and his brother called him back to live and work among the monks. Then he learned the spiritual value of work, which led him to understand community. He came to see that when he worked with his hands to serve a brother, the brother's acceptance of the gift brought him, as the giver, immediate joy. His gift also brought him the hope of a reward in heaven. His work was doubly blessed because he served his brother and at the same time served Christ present in his brother. He gave his love to the neighbor and to God at the same time. In intercessory prayer as well, love is shared with the one in need and with God simultaneously. So John's work proved to be the same kind of activity as intercessory prayer, though it was done with the hands instead of the mind.

Work in a community becomes a way of exchanging gifts. This means that receiving a gift is also a necessary part of the dance of shared life, because without a recipient no gift can be given. John knows well the blessings of work from his experience with his brother in their cell, and he does not want the priest to be deprived of these blessings. He wishes the priest joy, not

22. John the Dwarf 7; trans. Ward, *Sayings*, 86–87, alt.

grief. So he receives the priest's gift of something to drink. His reception of it is, in turn, a gift to the priest. By sharing a bodily meal, by serving each other with their hands as well as praying together, the monks are drawn into closer community than if they had prayed together without the meal. Their bodies, as well as their souls, brought the monks together.

7

In the Created World

What is humankind's relationship with animals and with the natural world? Since God made humans in his image, they have a privileged position vis-à-vis the other creatures of the earth. But what does this privilege mean? Does the widespread ecological destruction in the world today result from a belief that humans, because they are made in the image of God, exercise divinely mandated dominion over the earth and its creatures? And what does this "dominion" authorize them to do? Does this belief support human exploitation of animals and plants for our own selfish purposes? As a result of such exploitation, many species have already become extinct.

Science has shown how humans are connected with animals, plants, and the earth's ecosystem. If we poison the whole earth's environment with pollution, we ourselves will not have the resources to survive. We will have lost our only home. So are we just part of the earth's biology? Or, since we are made in God's image, are we different from other creatures even though we are profoundly connected to them?

Today these are pressing questions. God values his creation. He cares for the earth and all its creatures. If we are made in his

image and called to bear his likeness, surely we should care for
the earth and its creatures too. As we saw in the last chapter, our
connection with the natural world gives us the ability to mediate between God and the earth. This mediation is a key part of
our vocation as persons made in God's image. The saints, who
bear God's likeness, show us how to relate to animals and all
the world's creatures with love, not to exploit and destroy, but
to bring well-being and peace; not to create imbalance, but to
bring balance and stability.

As an example, let us see how Francis of Assisi, the twelfth-
century Italian saint, mediated between God, a savage wolf,
and the town of Gubbio. As Francis is staying in Gubbio, a wolf
comes and lurks in the woods outside the town's walls. It eats
both animals and people. Terrified, the townsfolk do not dare go
out there alone, and when they do go, they take weapons with
them. Francis has compassion for the people of Gubbio, so he
goes out to meet the wolf. He takes no weapons but makes the
sign of the cross and puts his trust in God. The townspeople
and his disciples watch from afar as he approaches the animal.
He sets out to make peace and calls the wolf his brother. This
is how the story was told in the Middle Ages:

> The wolf, seeing all this multitude, ran towards St. Francis with
> his jaws wide open. As he approached, the saint, making the sign
> of the cross, cried out: "Come here, brother wolf; I command
> you, in the name of Christ, neither to harm me nor anybody
> else."

The wolf closes his jaws, stops running, comes up to Francis, and
lies at his feet like a lamb. Then Francis speaks to him again:

> Brother wolf, you have done much evil in this land, destroying
> and killing the creatures of God without his permission; yes,
> not only animals have you destroyed, but you have even dared
> to devour people, made in the image of God; for which you
> are worthy of being hanged like a robber and a murderer. All
> people cry out against you, the dogs pursue you, and all the
> inhabitants of this city are your enemies; but I will make peace

between them and you, O brother wolf, if indeed you no longer offend them, and they will forgive you all your past offenses, and neither people nor dogs will pursue you any more.

In response, the wolf makes signs of submission to show his agreement. Francis then promises that the people of the city will feed him all his life if he keeps a promise never to attack any animal or human being. The wolf bows his head in assent. Then Francis asks him to make a pledge and stretches out his hand. The wolf puts his paw in Francis's hand, and they shake hands, ratifying the agreement.

After this, Francis asks the wolf to go with him into the town, and he walks meekly beside the saint into the marketplace, where the people are assembled. Francis preaches to them, warning that the flames of hell are worse than a wolf's jaws, so they must repent of their sins. He then asks them to promise to feed the wolf all his life and has the wolf re-enact his promise and handshake before all the townspeople. At this, everybody rejoices, and the town lives in peace with the wolf from then on.

> The wolf lived two years at Gubbio; he went familiarly from door to door without harming anyone, and all the people received him courteously, feeding him with great pleasure, and no dog barked at him as he went about. At last, after two years, he died of old age, and the people of Gubbio mourned his loss greatly; for when they saw him going about so gently among them all, he reminded them of the virtue and sanctity of St. Francis.[1]

In this story, Francis enacts the mediation that is his task as one made in the image of God. First, in order to mediate between God and the natural world, represented by the wolf, he has to understand and accept his intrinsic connection with the creation around him. So from the outset, he regards the wolf as his brother and treats him with heartfelt love. Francis is also connected with God. He prays and makes the sign of

1. *Fioretti di San Francesco* 21, in Roger Huddleston, ed., *The Little Flowers of Saint Francis of Assisi* (Springfield, IL: Templegate, 1988), 56–59, alt.

the cross, but clearly he lives his whole life in communion with God. This is why he is able to act as God's image to the wolf by speaking God's words with God's authority: "I command you, in the name of Christ, neither to harm me nor anybody else." The wolf's meek obedience shows that the mediation is genuine.

There are many stories of saints throughout the ages to whom wild animals are drawn and to whom they respond with gentleness and obedience. This is true of some of the desert fathers of fourth-century Egypt. Seraphim of Sarov, a nineteenth-century Russian saint, had a bear eat bread out of his hand, and he taught a frightened nun to feed the bear in the same way. The animals, as God's creatures, have their own relationships with their Creator in ways that we fallen humans do not know. It appears they can perceive God in the saints and recognize the saints' love for them, so they need not react with fear or hostility as they do with other humans. Perhaps they are restored to the way they related to humans in paradise before the fall. Like Adam giving names to the animals (see Gen. 2:19–20), Francis has a natural authority over the wolf. In turn, the wolf clearly recognizes and accepts this authority.

Once Francis has made himself a connecting link between God and the wolf, he is able to bring harmony to his whole environment by bringing the wolf and the people of Gubbio into right relationship with God and then with each other. He declares God's judgment to the wolf and asks him to repent, which the wolf does. Francis also preaches repentance to the townspeople, who likewise respond. The wolf must promise not to harm people or other animals, and since they were to provide the wolf with food, the people of Gubbio must promise to feed him.

Then, amazingly, the wolf takes on the character of St. Francis by remaining tame and meek. Francis's character comes from God, since he has followed Christ's example and, through grace, become like him. So Francis has received kindness, gentleness, and joy from Christ and has passed these virtues along to the wolf. Now as the wolf walks around the town looking for food, he is no longer an enemy. Every day he brings the townspeople the saint's gentleness, and they respond to the wolf with love.

In the twentieth century, local lore recounts that workers who were restoring the medieval church in Gubbio did some excavation. The bones of a wolf were found buried inside the church, in a place where ordinarily only people would be buried.[2] In the minds of Gubbio's townspeople, the reconciliation between humans and the wolf was complete.

Francis as Microcosm and Mediator

Francis participated in both the heavenly realm of souls and angels and the earthly realm of plants and animals. He united these two worlds, these two levels of reality, in himself and brought both into the presence of God. He also brought God to the world and its creatures around him. So the twelfth-century saint fulfilled the human vocation described by earlier Christian writers as that of *microcosm* and *mediator*.

The human person is able to connect with the different levels of reality in the universe because he or she already participates in them. The mind is able to perceive God, angels, and other human minds because it shares in spiritual reality, just as they do. The body is connected with every kind of reality in the physical universe, so we can perceive all these kinds of realities, either with our naked eyes or with the help of scientific instruments. Our bodies have received protons and electrons from star dust, atoms from the earth, organic molecules from the biosphere, and genes from the animals. So we share in all the levels of reality in the universe, but on a smaller scale. This means that the human person is a microcosm, or a small world.

Because he or she is a microcosm and thus connected with everything in the universe, the human is able to unite things with each other and with God. Part of being God's likeness is to serve as a *mediator*, just as Francis mediated between God and the wolf. To mediate is to bring God to the world in blessing and

2. Jim Forest, *The Ladder of the Beatitudes* (Maryknoll, NY: Orbis, 1999), 118.

to bring the world to God in receptivity and thanksgiving. So Christ blessed the wolf, and the wolf received Christ's gentleness. In this way, Francis exemplified the *royal priesthood* (see 1 Pet. 2:9) to which every human person is called, including lay people. This ministry also means bringing into harmony different parts of the created world. Thus Francis also mediated between the wolf and the townspeople of Gubbio.

The Human Person as Microcosm and Mediator

To understand the human vocation as microcosm and mediator, let us consider what two early Christian theologians, Gregory of Nazianzus and Maximus the Confessor, have to say about it.

Gregory of Nazianzus

Gregory explains how, in his view, God built the structure of the universe and then created humankind within it to fulfill the vocation of microcosm and mediator. He first provides the context by explaining how God was motivated by goodness to create the world. God is so good that he wants to share his goodness with others. It was not sufficient for him to gaze at his own goodness and delight in it, for his great goodness had to expand beyond himself. In other words, "it was not sufficient for goodness to be moved only in contemplation of itself," as Gregory says, "but it was necessary that the good be poured forth and spread outward, so that there would be more recipients of its benevolent activity, for this was the summit of goodness."[3]

Gregory then says that God created the spiritual realm first and the earthly realm second. He speaks of each as illumined by God, because the Creator shares his light with all he has made. In this text, Gregory attempts to describe the angels, though he admits it is difficult. Everything is created by the three persons of the Trinity, he says, and they create effortlessly as divine thoughts are transformed into divine actions.

3. *Oration* 38.9; trans. Harrison, *St. Gregory,* 66–67.

Therefore [God the Father] first thought of the angelic and heavenly powers, and the thought was action, accomplished by the Word and perfected by the Spirit. And thus were created the second radiances, the servants of the first Radiance, which are either intelligent spirits, or a kind of immaterial and bodiless fire, or some other nature as close to those just mentioned as possible. I would like to say that they are unmoved toward evil and have only the movement toward the good, since they are around God and are the first to be illumined by God; for things here below are illumined second.[4]

Because the angels orbit around God and share his illumination, as it were, Gregory calls them "second radiances." Nevertheless, as he goes on to admit, Lucifer and his followers fell into evil.

Because Gregory is discussing the process of creation, the origin of evil is a digression. As damaging as evil is, God's work and purpose in creating are good. Gregory then says that God delighted in the immaterial realm of the angels, so he went on to create another world, the one familiar to us, the universe that is our home.

And since the first world was beautiful to God, he thought a second material and visible world, that which is composed of heaven and earth and the system and composite of realities existing between them. It is praiseworthy because of the good orientation of each thing, but more praiseworthy because of the good connectedness and harmony of the whole, as each thing is well adapted to another and all to all, into the full realization of one world.[5]

Like the Stoic philosophers, Gregory here describes the beauty of the material universe in terms of its organization, the harmony of its parts, and the ways those parts fit together. This world includes the heavens—that is, the sun, moon, stars, and the vast spaces around them—as well as the earth and all its creatures.

4. *Oration* 38.9; trans. Harrison, *St. Gregory*, 67.
5. *Oration* 38.10; trans. Harrison, *St. Gregory*, 67.

So at this stage in God's creative work, there are two worlds: one spiritual and the other material. Both are good and beautiful, but they remain separate and do not communicate with each other. Because the angelic world can be perceived by the mind and the material world can be perceived by sense perception, the missing link will be the one creature who possesses both mind and sense perception and can thus mediate communication between the two worlds. That creature is the human being. According to Gregory, the human being who joins together the two worlds by participating in both is God's masterpiece. Imagine an arch with a column of stones on each side. The fullest expression of the builder's art will be the keystone at the top, which fits well with each column yet joins the two together.

Gregory explains the creation and identity of the human being as follows:

> Thus far mind and sense perception . . . remained within their own limits and bore in themselves the magnificence of the Creator Word. They silently praised the greatness of his works and were heralds sounding afar [Ps. 19:3–4]. But there was not yet a blending out of both, nor a mixing of opposites, which is the distinctive sign of a greater wisdom and of divine superabundance concerning created natures, nor was the full wealth of goodness yet made known. So then wishing to manifest this, the Creator Word also makes one living creature out of both, I mean invisible and visible natures, that is, the human being. And having taken the body from the matter already created, he breathed in breath from himself [Gen. 2:7], which is surely the intelligent soul and the image of God of which Scripture speaks [see Gen. 1:26–27]. The human being is a kind of second world, great in smallness, placed on the earth, another angel, a composite worshiper, a beholder of the visible creation, an initiate into the intelligible, king of things on earth, subject to what is above, earthly and heavenly, transitory and immortal, visible and intelligible, a mean between greatness and lowliness. He is at once spirit and flesh.[6]

6. *Oration* 38.11; trans. Harrison, *St. Gregory*, 68.

According to Genesis 2:7, the human person is created from earth and God's breath, so from the outset his or her very being combines elements of both worlds. Gregory calls the human person "a second world, great in smallness," which paraphrases and further explains the word "microcosm." Humans are second because they are created after the world, and despite their small size by comparison with the whole universe, Gregory affirms that they have great status and value because they are God's image.

Humans' home is on the earth, but, as God originally created them, their function and activities, the most important of which is worship, are the same as those of the angels. Thus humans live in the material world and have material bodies, but Gregory calls the human person "another angel." Humans' participation in the material world is essential to their work of mediation and makes them "composite worshipers," both spiritual and material, who perceive and share in both worlds. Thus the human being is earthly, transitory, and visible to eyes, yet is also heavenly, immortal, and perceived by mind.

Our task, then, is to live harmonious lives, holding together the parts of ourselves that connect us with different parts of creation. As we struggle for harmony within ourselves, we are also contributing to the accomplishment of a much larger task: bringing harmony to the whole creation. We are called to worship God on behalf of the created universe, but we are also called to become peacemakers within the vast and varied creation. "Blessed are the peacemakers, for they will be called children of God" (Matt. 5:9 NRSV).

Maximus the Confessor

Maximus, a seventh-century monk who was a profound theologian, studied Gregory of Nazianzus carefully and even wrote commentaries on difficult points in his writings. Maximus further developed Gregory's idea of the human person as microcosm and mediator. Because of his all-embracing vision of the human person's place in the universe, we will look at his understanding of human mediation.

Maximus believes that the human person was created with the vocation of bridging five divisions in the universe. This bridging means bringing together, not eradicating, such opposite extremes as heaven and earth. The human could have done this by following the path of monastic life to its ultimate goal, that is, by fully practicing virtues and contemplation. But because of the fall, people failed in this task. So Christ, who is the divine Word, became human and accomplished the task on our behalf, though he did so in a different way. So now people can share in Christ's work of mediation, and thus their original vocation is restored. Maximus's explanation of how this works is a bit complicated, so I will summarize it in a table and then provide an explanation.[7]

Five Mediations

Divisions	Human task	Christ's task
1. male/female	fullness of virtue	virgin birth
2. paradise/inhabited earth	love of God and neighbors	saves good thief; resurrection appearances
3. earth/heaven (or sky)	freedom from earthly attachments, angelic peace	ascension
4. material world/ spiritual world	contemplation of created realities	further ascension
5. creation/God; created/Uncreated	loving contemplation	seated with the Father

The first division is between male and female, and this probably needs more explanation than the others. As a monk, Maximus was of course celibate. He always writes from a monastic perspective, and those for whom he is writing are also monks. He presupposes that the way of life for monks and nuns is the same. It involves working to develop the universally human potential for virtue and contemplation, that is, love of neighbor and love of God, and thereby coming to share the life of

7. This section is based on Maximus, *Difficulty* 41; trans. Louth, *Maximus*, 156–62. I have also relied on explanations by Louth, *Maximus*, 72–74, 155–56, and Lars Thunberg's classic study *Microcosm and Mediator: The Theological Anthropology of Maximus the Confessor*, 2nd ed. (Chicago: Open Court, 1995), 373–429.

angels. Struggling against disordered desires and emotions is the monk's first task. This means moving away from an unbalanced life and toward a wholeness that actualizes the human potential of practicing all the virtues. According to Maximus, this first task of acquiring virtues is where the division between male and female is overcome. Today we tend to think of masculinity and femininity as unequivocally good, whereas Maximus is thinking of their limitations. Yet he always thinks of sanctification as involving a reorientation, not an eradication, of human qualities that have been misused in sin.

In the Greco-Roman Empire, and in the Byzantine Empire that it had become by the seventh century, there were prejudices about men and women. In people's minds, maleness was associated with assertiveness and femaleness with desire, although these are human impulses that everybody possesses.[8] So when people are out of balance and there is too much emphasis on one of these impulses, men can become too macho and women too sensuous. Then conflict arises between them. The solution is for each side to move from stereotypical masculinity or femininity toward human balance and wholeness.

In addition, sometimes certain virtues were considered masculine, such as courage, while others were considered feminine, such as nurturing. The same ideas exist today. So if men had only the masculine virtues, they would be missing those ascribed to women, and vice versa. Yet the aim of spiritual growth is to acquire and practice *all* the virtues and thus to arrive at human wholeness. Especially in monastic life, this means developing good qualities associated with both genders. From this point of view, being restricted to the moral excellence of one gender or the other would impose a limitation that must be overcome in order to progress in the spiritual journey. So Maximus says that the division between male and female is overcome by "the most dispassionate relationship to divine virtue."[9]

8. See my explanation of human emotions and impulses in chapter 4.
9. *Difficulty* 41; trans. Louth, *Maximus*, 157.

What does this mean for people today? Perhaps for us the first division to be bridged is the prejudice that divides people from one another on the basis of gender but also race, class, ethnicity, culture, and disability. If we are to love our neighbors, we have to recognize that in the first place all of them are human beings, just as we are. So we do have things to share with them, just as they can share with us. In our different experiences of life, each of us has had to develop different virtues. So we can learn from those who differ from us how to become more fully human. This is the way we manifest more virtues, more of God's likeness.

The second division we face, according to Maximus, is the gap between paradise and the inhabited earth, or the civilized world he knows. Notice that this means he believes paradise is on earth, not up in the clouds somewhere. Our world is divided from paradise by the fall; we and our society are sinful, so we are definitely outside paradise. In fact, paradise is less a place than a way of life. If all people were saints and shared a profound peace with each other, perhaps we would be living in paradise. So, according to Maximus, the way to bridge the gap between the world we know and paradise is to love God as a community with all our heart, soul, mind, and strength and to love our neighbors as ourselves (see Mark 12:30–31). If everybody did this, the division between our world and paradise would disappear. This is the aim of monastic community life.

The third division is between earth and sky within our material universe. Having overcome passions, practiced virtues, and arrived at peace with other people, the human person is asked to serve as cosmic mediator. The first gap to be bridged is the vast difference between earth and the heavens, that is, the sky, sun, moon, and stars. In monastic life, this stage represents the transition from a focus on the struggle for virtues—though this struggle remains throughout one's life—to a focus on contemplation. Contemplation requires detachment. In other words, the monk (or nun) must detach from material possessions, from the exclusive focus on bodily needs here and now on earth, in order to be open to a broader perspective. Then one can begin to truly see and contemplate the whole material universe, including the stars. For Maximus, perception can establish unity by linking the observer to the reality observed. So the one who contemplates the whole material universe becomes the focal point at which it is all united. The stars find their unity with the earth within the human person, and more specifically, within the human body. If we remember that the atoms of the human body are composed of star dust, this connection begins to make sense. Another factor that contributes to this cosmic unity is that the monk has arrived at peace similar to the peace of the angels. This peace, like the peace of St. Francis, helps to draw things around oneself into harmony, wholeness, and unity.

The fourth division is between the material world, what is perceived through the senses, and the spiritual world, what is perceived through the mind. To bridge this gap, the perception of the senses and the perception of the mind have to be merged. As a result, a new kind of unity occurs within the human person that enables unity between the two worlds. These are the same two worlds that Gregory of Nazianzus spoke about. Maximus believes that this merging occurs when the monk contemplates nature. This kind of contemplation enables one to see a material object and at the same time see within it the principle according to which God created it. This principle reveals what the object truly is and the purpose toward which it is heading. It also reveals the object's connection with other things, that is, its connection with its environment and perhaps with the universe as a whole. Again, the person who has this kind of perception becomes the focal point for cosmic unification, according to Maximus. The union between one's body and soul, manifested in that person perceiving through eyes and mind simultaneously, is a microcosm of union between the material and spiritual worlds.

If the fourth division is mysterious because it refers to a kind of contemplation few people today have experienced, the fifth and last division is even more mysterious. How can the division between everything that has been created and God the Creator be bridged? In fact, only God, through grace, can initiate this unification. For Maximus this union is the summit of all human experience. It involves contemplation of God, which surpasses all human understanding. This is how Maximus describes it:

> And finally, . . . the human person unites the created nature with the uncreated through love—O the wonder of God's love for us human beings! This shows them to be one and the same through the possession of grace, as the whole creation is wholly interpenetrated by God, and becomes completely whatever God is, except at the level of being. And the whole creation receives to itself the whole of God himself, and acquires, as a kind of prize for its ascent to God, the most unique God himself.[10]

Thus through the ultimate mediation of the perfected human person, God shares what he is with the whole of creation and dwells within it as fully as he dwells in himself. The difference is that the being of created things remains created even when they are filled with God, whereas God's own being is divine. In this passage, Maximus attempts to describe deification. He refers to a kind of divine presence far greater than the way God is present throughout the universe as the Maker of everything. Perhaps he is really thinking of the eschaton. The Creator's presence in the cosmos now points forward to this absolute fullness of God's indwelling in the age to come. "For the earth will be filled with the knowledge of the glory of the LORD, as the waters cover the sea" (Hab. 2:14).

To mediate God's deifying presence to the created world is the utmost fulfillment of the cosmic priesthood, a role for which we were created as the image and likeness of God. Yet, as Maximus acknowledges, through our fallenness we have failed to complete the process he describes. God must always complete the last step—deification—but we have failed to achieve even the first step, the fullness of virtues. So how is God's intention for the created world to be fulfilled? As Maximus says, God completes the task of human royal priesthood

---

10. *Difficulty* 41; trans. Louth, *Maximus*, 158, alt.

himself through the incarnation. Yet the steps he takes are different from the ones we would have taken to become perfect monks or nuns.

Christ overcomes the division between male and female, according to Maximus, by being born of a virgin. Though ordinarily one parent of each gender is needed to procreate, all of Christ's humanity comes from his virgin mother. She must have possessed a wholeness that bridges the gap between the capacities of both male and female, and she passed along this human wholeness to her Son.

He overcomes the other four divisions later, at the time of his death, resurrection, and ascension. As he was hanging on the cross, one of the thieves beside him admitted his own guilt and confessed faith in Jesus. Jesus says to him, "Today you will be with me in Paradise" (Luke 23:43). The thief crossed the bridge Jesus built from the inhabited earth to paradise, since the thief immediately went to paradise when he died. Jesus also bridged the gap when he died. Then, after his resurrection, he came back across that bridge to his disciples and showed them his risen body, which was already living the life of paradise.

By his ascension, Christ in his human flesh passes from earth, the body's home, through the sky and through the spiritual world, the realm of the angels. In this way, he bridges the third and fourth divisions, namely, those between earth and heaven and between the material and spiritual worlds. Finally, as human he sits at the right hand of the Father, on the same throne as God. This is how he overcomes the final gap between the created world and God.

Christ has restored the human vocation of cosmic priesthood. By his grace, and in union with him, people are empowered to bring harmony and unity to the created world and to bestow God's blessing on creation while offering creation back to God in thanksgiving. Christ's way of accomplishing this task, according to Maximus, differed from the way of the perfect monk (or nun) he describes. St. Francis may have found yet another way. Since God is very creative, he guides people by many ways to fulfill this vocation.

Healing God's Creatures

To complete this chapter, let us look at three contemporary examples of how the cosmic vocation of the divine image has been fulfilled: (1) a country veterinarian, (2) the work of many people to save an endangered species, and (3) the blessing of an inner-city lake.

A Country Veterinarian

James Herriot was a country veterinarian in the north of England. He practiced in a small town, serving the local pets, the farm animals in the surrounding countryside, and the people who cared for them or depended on them for their livelihood. He was a keen observer of people, animals, and their relationships. His loving heart and gentle, skilled hands reached out to all of them, in whatever way he could. He wrote down his observations in a series of books that describe the whole world in which he lived. They became best sellers, and though he did not know it, he offered the example of his love for animals and people to millions of readers.

I will tell only one of his many stories. Once he spent a long afternoon working with pigs at a farm so that when he left it was already dark. As he was driving home on a country road, a big car passed him, turned around, came back, and stopped. The driver waved frantically to him, so he also stopped. The family in the big car was on a road trip. Their dog Benny had swallowed a little rubber ball that lodged in his throat and blocked his windpipe. They went to Herriot's office and then came out again to look for him. The father had tried to get the ball out but could not, and the dog, a lovely collie, had stopped breathing. The mother sat in the front seat crying silently. In the back, the four children were upset. "Oh, Benny, Benny, Benny!" they said, and, "Oh daddy, he's dead, he's dead!"

The father and the veterinarian took Benny from the children and laid him in front of the car so they could see him in the headlights. Then, as Herriot explains, he got to work:

I pushed my hand into the mouth and I could feel it all right. A sphere of hard solid rubber not much bigger than a golf ball and jammed like a cork in the pharynx, effectively blocking the trachea. I scrabbled feverishly at the wet smoothness but there was nothing to get hold of. It took me about three seconds to realize that no human agency would ever get the ball out that way and without thinking I withdrew my hands, braced both thumbs behind the angle of the lower jaw and pushed.

The ball shot forth like a cork from a champagne bottle and rolled away. But alas, the collie was still not breathing. He looked dead. Herriot regretted that he had not been there sooner, but he discovered that the heart was still beating. He had no stimulant injections or oxygen canisters with him, so, as he says, "I began to work on the dog with all I had." He gave the dog artificial respiration, pressing his palms rhythmically on Benny's chest and blowing into his throat. His heart continued to beat, and in time his eyelids twitched and he lifted his own ribs to breathe. As the artificial respiration continued, his breathing became deep and regular, and he became aware of his surroundings. Then, as Herriot stood up, the dog also staggered to his feet.

The young father was stunned, but the children in the back seat squealed with delight. As the car drove away, they had their arms around their beloved pet and cried out, "Benny . . . Benny . . . Benny . . ." After the fact, Herriot reflected on what had happened: "When you know without a shadow of a doubt that, even without doing anything clever, you have pulled an animal back from the brink of death into the living, breathing world, it is a satisfaction which lingers."[11] The veterinarian, with his medical skill and experience, mediated life to the collie. He supported Benny's lungs with his hands and shared his own breath with the dog. By saving the dog, he brought a whole family of humans to shared joy.

11. James Herriot, *All Things Wise and Wonderful* (New York: St. Martin's Press, 1977), 67–70.

Saving an Endangered Species

I grew up in Los Angeles, in the northwest corner of the San Fernando Valley, just over the hills from the California condor's habitat in Ventura County. When I was a child, my father told me of times he could see the magnificent black birds flying overhead, and he hoped that I would see one too. I never did, perhaps because so few of them were left. As I grew older, I learned they were an endangered species.

The condors are the largest birds native to North America, and it is glorious to see one in flight. Journalist John Nielsen describes them as follows:

> The California condor is a New World vulture with telescopic eyes, a razor-sharp beak, and a wingspan of nearly ten feet. Helicopter pilots say they've seen it soaring well above ten thousand feet. I have seen it glide for miles without ever bothering to flap. Condors never show the wobbly V shape you see on smaller, lesser vultures. The giant black wings form a horizontal line that's often mistaken for an airplane. The thick black feathers at the ends of these wings are nearly two feet long.[12]

Condors flourished in the Pleistocene era, when they ate mastodons,[13] and have survived ever since. In 1979, however, only twenty-five to thirty-five remained alive in the world.[14] In the twentieth century, field biologists quietly studied them and learned a lot about their habitat and way of life. In the wild they reproduce slowly, laying one egg every two years. But many lost their lives due to shooting, poison, being caught in traps, or flying into power lines.[15] In the early twentieth century, people stole many of their large pale-blue eggs because they had become valuable collector's items.

12. John Nielsen, *Condor: To the Brink and Back—the Life and Times of One Giant Bird* (New York: Harper Perennial, 2006), 1. There is a video of a condor in flight at the website http://cacondorconservation.org (accessed July 21, 2008).
13. Nielsen, *Condor*, 1.
14. www.sandiegozoo.org/conservation/ (accessed May 9, 2009).
15. Nielsen, *Condor*, 144.

In 1979, biologists warned that the best way to save them would be to capture all the remaining condors, keep them in zoos, and breed them. This plan was controversial because of the risk that all of them would be lost if it did not work. There was also a worry that condors raised in zoos might not be able to survive in the wild. Nevertheless, it was the last available option to save them. In 1980, a team of scientists and naturalists was assembled to do whatever they could to preserve the bird from extinction. Their plans were ambitious, a "long-term large-scale program involving a greatly increased research effort, immediate steps to identify and conserve vast areas of suitable condor habitat, *and* captive propagation."[16]

All surviving condors were captured and taken to the San Diego Zoo. Shortly before this step was taken, field biologists had discovered that if a condor loses an egg, she will lay another one the same season. So the zoo keepers took one egg from each mother bird and raised it separately, letting her care for the second one. They also found that in captivity, the birds would lay eggs every year instead of every other year. So the zoos have been able to increase the population. They have also been careful about preparing birds to return to the wild and survive there. Humans who raise chicks wear condor puppets on their hands so the young birds will learn to trust their own kind and not depend on humans.

Now condors are kept in several zoos. Colonies have been released into the wild in Ventura County, their last surviving native habitat, and also in places where they once lived, such as in Arizona near the Grand Canyon and in Baja California, Mexico. The birds are watched carefully; every bird has a tag with a number. Those that are released are given electronic homing devices, so scientists can track where they go and find out what hazards they encounter. Every so often they are captured, given medical care, and released again. If they do poorly in the wild, they are brought back to the zoo.

16. Nielsen, *Condor*, 149–50, emphasis in the original. He is quoting "a panel of prominent scientists."

Hundreds of people have collaborated on this team effort. The funding has come from government agencies and nonprofit organizations. The plan is still underway, and there are still risks, but so far it has been successful. "As of May 2008, there are 332 California condors, with 152 of those birds living in the wild."[17]

Sanford Wilbur, the man who headed the California condor recovery effort for the US Fish and Wildlife Service in 1979 and recommended the radical step of taking all surviving condors to zoos for breeding, is a Christian. He considered his work a vocation, "taking care of something God made." The condors did not serve any particular human need, but they belonged to God. Wilbur said he worked to "develop a process for saving condors that emphasized cooperation, integrity, and credibility."[18] He did not see himself as "playing God," but he accepted the sacred trust of helping God care for his creation. Together with all his colleagues, he was fulfilling the task of one made in God's likeness. He surely believed that since humans had disturbed the condors' habitat and threatened their existence, humans had the responsibility to intervene again proactively to rescue the birds and restore their habitat.

The Blessing of an Inner-City Lake

The Orthodox Church celebrates a feast day called Theophany, which means "Manifestation of God," on January 6th. It focuses on Christ's baptism in the Jordan River. It is a chance for each of the faithful to be renewed in the grace of his or her baptism, which was a cleansing from sin and a renewal. The feast also celebrates the Holy Trinity, since, according to Scripture, Christ's baptism is the first time the Trinity is explicitly revealed. The Son incarnate stands in the water; the Father speaks from heaven, saying, "This is my beloved Son"; and the Holy Spirit descends upon Christ in the form of a dove (see Matt. 3:16–17).

17. See www.sandiegozoo.org/conservation/ (accessed May 9, 2009).
18. Nielsen, Condor, 143–44.

Yet there is a another meaning to Theophany that has profound ecological significance. Jesus was baptized for a number of reasons, but, according to Gregory of Nazianzus, one purpose was "to sanctify the Jordan."[19] Because he was God incarnate, he did not need to be cleansed by the water; rather, the presence of his body cleansed the water. Any evil lurking within it was destroyed. So Christ's baptism is the origin of the holy water in which all Christians are baptized. In the Orthodox baptismal service, there is a prayer that the person being baptized will receive "the blessing of Jordan."

On Theophany there is a service called the Great Blessing of Water, in which the church imitates what Christ did in his baptism. This service is done twice. The first time it is done in the church to bless holy water. The second time it is done outdoors, to bless the water that is the fundamental element of the earth's ecosystem. Orthodox Christians do this around the world. On Greek islands, the congregation goes down to the beach and blesses the ocean. In Alaska—remember, this is January—the priest cuts a hole in the ice and blesses the water beneath it. At St. Nicholas Church in San Anselmo, California, the congregation walks in procession to the creek that flows through the small town and blesses it. The creek, which has now become holy water, flows down into the San Francisco Bay and from there into the Pacific Ocean. The water blessed at Theophany carries God's blessing to everything it touches, that is, to the whole natural world. At this service, the faithful pray for the water and through it for the earth's whole biosphere.

If people bless a creek every year, they are less likely to pollute it. If the blessed water is already polluted, it may be cleaned up. Once for Theophany I went to the urban parish of St. Mary of Egypt Church in Kansas City. We went to bless Troost Lake, which is in an inner-city park near the church. One of the parishioners told me they had been blessing it for several years. During that time, he said, the city had cleaned up the lake. The old, rusted automobiles and other trash had been removed from the

19. *Oration* 39.15; trans. Harrison, *St. Gregory*, 91.

water, and recently he had been fishing in that lake. He caught a healthy fish there and was able to eat it. So God answered their prayers: he bestowed his blessing, and people cleared the pollution away. At Theophany, the priest, and with him every member of the congregation, act as mediators, bringing God's blessing to the natural world.

Conclusion

Because humans are made in the divine image, they possess the capacities to use reason, priestly mediation, and royal power in their relationships with the natural world. Reason enables scientists to observe, study, and understand the earth and its creatures. This scientific work supports care for God's creation, such as James Herriot's practice of healing animals and through them the families that love them and depend on them. Science also provided Sanford Wilbur and all his colleagues with insight into the condor and its environmental needs so they could save it from extinction.

Priestly mediation enabled St. Francis to offer brother wolf to God and bestow God's blessing on him. It enabled him to establish covenant relationships between God and the wolf and between the wolf and the townspeople. The congregation that prayed for Troost Lake at Theophany and bestowed God's blessing on it also exercised the royal priesthood that belongs to every human person made in God's image.

But what are we to make of the authority inherent in the divine image? In Genesis 1:26, God says, "Let us make human-kind in our image, according to our likeness; and let them have dominion over the fish of the sea, and over the birds of the air, and over the cattle, and over all the earth" (NRSV).[20] In this chapter we have seen several examples of this dominion being used to aid and bless animals. St. Francis used it to order the wolf, in the name of Jesus Christ, not to harm anyone. This

---

20. I have incorporated the alternative reading that the NRSV lists in a footnote as a translation from the Syriac, "all the earth." This reading is also found in the RSV.

was for the wolf's benefit, as his compliance kept the people
of Gubbio from killing him and allowed them to feed him for
as long as he lived.

The team that saved the condors also had to use consider-
able authority to achieve their aim, including the authority of
government. The state legislature had to appropriate funds to
support their conservation efforts and pass laws to protect the
condors' habitat. But these are laws aimed at guiding *human*
behavior, not bird behavior. In addition, the biologists, field
hands, and zoo keepers had to capture all the surviving condors
and hold them in captivity in zoos in order to save them. They
track them with electronic sensors, catch them periodically
for medical treatment, then release them again. To do these
things for the condors' benefit, they have to continually exercise the dominion named in Genesis 1:26 over the birds of the
air. The decision of humans to interfere in the birds' lives was
controversial at the time it was made. Some environmentalists
did not want such human intrusion. But the program has been
successful, and similar programs are now in place to save other
endangered species.

Because we are made in God's image, we humans are interconnected with every part of the universe, especially every
part of the earth's biosphere, and we have power that reaches
throughout the created world. Basil wrote about this power
through examples of hunters using their skill to capture lions,
birds, and large sea creatures.[21] Today these examples are pain-
ful to read. We forget that in his time, the animals really had
a chance against hunters. Basil had a younger brother named
Naucratius who was not an intellectual like Basil and Gregory of
Nyssa but became a hermit living and praying in the woods. He
used his skill in hunting to provide food for some elderly people
who lived nearby. But he died young in a hunting accident. His
example inspired Basil to become a monk and start a monastic community.[22] But today land animals and fish do not have a

---

21. *On the Origin of Humanity* 1.9–10; trans. Harrison, *St. Basil*, 37–39.
22. See Gregory of Nyssa's account in the *Life of St. Macrina*; trans. Callahan,
Gregory of Nyssa, esp. 168–69.

chance against hunters who use night vision goggles and rifles or fishermen with large mechanized boats and sonar.

Human power over the natural world has grown much greater over time. Through sin we have misused this power, exploiting the earth's ecosystem for our own selfish gain instead of caring for it. Yet the power itself is rooted in the divine image that makes us human. This is why we have had the capacity to damage the environment as much as we have. Yet God has given humans the power, and so our power is inescapable. However, we are accountable to God for how we use it. We must decide how to redirect it toward good purposes. We can use it to support God's creative work by cleaning up the environment, bringing harmony to the earth, and safeguarding endangered species.

8

Arts and Sciences

In this book we have seen how, according to early Christians, the image of God present in each of us defines who we most truly are as humans. The divine image draws us toward the goal for which we were created; it draws us toward the life to come when God's image can shine forth in us most fully as our true identity, that is, toward union with God. This perspective raises questions about the place of culture in human identity and existence. Because of such questions, some monastics have renounced creativity and culture for the sake of single-minded pursuit of God's kingdom.

Early Christians believed that in the age to come, God, or Christ, will take the place of most of the things we need and pursue in our present lives. In the next life, Christ will become food for human souls as well as for angels. He will become the home in which people are sheltered, and he will also dwell within them. He will be the radiant robe in which people are clothed. So, once all this is fully accomplished, people will no longer be occupied with finding food, shelter, or clothing. Christ will have superseded all these things and will provide what is needed more perfectly than the things we seek in this life can provide. What, then, will become of human culture, which is built around finding, preserving, and sharing earthly things?

If God will take the place of everything, are the creativity and culture we value so highly today merely distractions, or are they truly human characteristics? Do they have authentic value? And what about the arts and sciences, the fruit of creativity and the pinnacle of culture, which are believed to represent the highest achievements of what is specifically human? Are they not expressions of the image of God in us?

This chapter will suggest that the achievements of culture, the arts, and the sciences do manifest the divine image in us and that our creation in the image of God in fact makes them possible. To be sure, cultural achievements can be misused, as can other human gifts, but they can also be used to lead us to God, which is the primary purpose of our creation in the divine image. Let us begin by considering a few distinguished scientists who found God through their studies of the natural world.

Because science and art are practiced and understood differently in modern times than they were in Late Antiquity, the examples in this chapter will be more recent. We will consider Johannes Kepler, who was born in the sixteenth century and lived during the rise of modern science, and Albert Einstein, the great twentieth-century physicist. Then we will consider the arts and focus on the example of Leonid Ouspensky, a twentieth-century iconographer who had modern sensibilities but belonged to an artistic tradition known to John of Damascus in the eighth century.

Kepler and God's Geometry

In March 2009, NASA launched a new space telescope. Over a period of three and a half years, it will have scanned the one-hundred-thousand stars nearest our solar system to see if there is evidence of planets like earth in other solar systems, planets with water that could support life.[1] Scientists at NASA have named this instrument the Kepler telescope, after the mathematician and astronomer Johannes Kepler (1571–1630).[2] Kepler was the first to discover the laws of planetary motion. Today's astronomers will see how these laws apply to the images of stars the new telescope will record, so as to calculate which of their planets may support life.

Kepler was born into poverty and died poor, though during his life he was a professor of mathematics, worked with the distinguished Danish astronomer Tycho Brahe, and served as court astronomer or mathematician to several German princes. He was a Lutheran who could not receive communion because in conscience he could not sign the Lutheran statement of faith, but neither could he bring himself to become a Catholic. As a result, he was alienated from both churches. So as a college student he had to give up his ambition of becoming a pastor. With the help of an inspiring teacher, he turned to mathematics and astronomy instead, but he never lost his interest in theology. During his life, the Thirty Years War between Lutherans and Catholics raged in Germany, and he had to move from place to place to escape the violence. Despite all these difficulties, he was able to publish a number of books that explained his groundbreaking scientific discoveries.

His contemporary Galileo (1564–1642) had recently declared that the sun, not the earth, was the center of our solar system. Kepler agreed with Galileo and worked to observe and calculate how the planets move around the sun. At first he sought to figure out the movements of the planets using mathematics supported by theology. He declared that they moved in perfect circles, representing the perfection of God. Yet as a pioneer of the modern scientific method, he always checked his theories against actual measurements of objects observed in the sky.

1. See John Johnson Jr., "NASA's Kepler Seeks Another Earth among the Stars," *Los Angeles Times*, March 6, 2009, www.latimes.com/news/nationworld/nation/la-na-kepler6–2009mar06,0,5238456.story (accessed March 7, 2009).

2. See NASA's discussion of Johannes Kepler and the telescope mission at http://kepler.nasa.gov (accessed March 7, 2009).

After much labor, he concluded that the orbit of Mars is not a circle but an ellipse and that the same is also true of the other planets.

Besides correlating scientific theory and experimental evidence, he also correlated science and theology throughout his writings. So he decided he needed to find a new theological justification for the elliptical orbits. He reasoned that a circle alone would have represented God, but a straight line represents created things. An ellipse, however, combines both, so the data he discovered proved to be theologically appropriate after all. To him the ellipse symbolized both the planets and their Creator, who was made manifest through them.

Kepler went on to formulate three mathematical laws of planetary motion that scientists, like those working with the new space telescope, still use today. In addition, he made major contributions to optics, and in mathematics he contributed to the study of logarithms, geometry, and calculus. He was the first to discover that the tides are caused by the moon's gravitational pull on the water and that the sun rotates on its axis. He also invented the word "satellite."[3]

If Kepler had become a Lutheran pastor, he would probably have been forgotten, and it might have taken others much longer to make the same scientific discoveries. Looking back on his early life, he observed, "I had the intention of being a theologian. For a long time I was restless, but now see how God is, by my endeavors, also glorified in astronomy."[4] Yet in his scientific work he remained a theologian. As an astronomer, he traced out how the skies were constructed, noting how orderly the Creator's work is. "God, like a master builder," he said, "has laid the foundation of the world according to law and order."[5]

3. On Kepler's life and work, see Nancy K. Frankenberry, *The Faith of Scientists in Their Own Words* (Princeton, NJ: Princeton University Press, 2008), 34–58. See also the websites http://kepler.nasa.gov/johannes and www.johanneskepler.com (both accessed March 7, 2009).

4. This was the dedication of Kepler's first book, *Mysterium Cosmographicum* (Tübingen: Georg Gruppenbach, 1596), translated and cited by Frankenberry, *Faith of Scientists*, 38–39.

5. Translated in Frankenberry, *Faith of Scientists*, 37.

He added that "those laws are within the grasp of the human mind; God wanted us to recognize them by creating us after his own image so that we could share in his own thoughts."[6] For Kepler, the connection between the divine model and its image in the human mind is what enables humans to grasp how God has structured the creation. Elsewhere, he calls the thought patterns in God's mind by which he structured the skies "geometry." Following medieval theologians, Kepler presupposes that the thoughts in God's mind are eternal and are included in God's own being. "Geometry," he writes, "which before the origin of things was coeternal with the divine mind and is God himself, supplied God with patterns for the creation of the world, and passed over to [the human being] along with the image of God."[7] Geometry is thus included in God's image, the human mind, as well. Kepler has made a bold statement here. He is saying that both the mathematical way of thinking that is the foundation of modern science and the human ability to do the scientific work itself derive directly from God and are included in the divinely created definition of what it is to be human.

In a letter to Baron von Herberstein, perhaps a potential benefactor, Kepler explains the value of his scientific work. He compares it to the arts, noting that like artistic expression, scientific discovery brings joy, though it does not have direct economic utility.

> One will ask, what is the good of the knowledge of nature, of all astronomy, to a hungry stomach? . . . Painters are allowed to go on with their work because they give joy to the eyes, musicians because they bring joy to the ears, though they are of no other use to us. . . . What insensibility, what stupidity, to deny the spirit an honest pleasure but permit it to the eyes and ears! He who fights against this joy fights against nature. . . . Should . . . the kind Creator who brought forth nature out of nothing . . . deprive the spirit of a human, the master of creation and the

6. Kepler, *Letter from Graz*; trans. Frankenberry, *Faith of Scientists*, 45.
7. Kepler, *The Harmony of the World*; trans. Frankenberry, *Faith of Scientists*, 37; see also 55–56.

Lord's own image, of every heavenly delight? Do we ask what profit the little bird hopes for in singing? We know that singing in itself is a joy to him because he was created for singing. We must not ask therefore why the human spirit takes such trouble to find out the secrets of the skies. Our Creator has given us a spirit in addition to the senses, for another reason than merely to provide a living for ourselves.[8]

Here Kepler argues that while the arts appeal to the senses, science appeals to the human mind or spirit.[9] He presupposes, following earlier theologians, that the mind or spirit is made in God's image and thus is master of creation. Hence it is natural to us as humans to seek understanding of creation, that is, to engage in scientific inquiries. And doing what is natural to us brings joy.

He adds that this work of discovery is God's will for human beings:

Our Creator wishes us to push ahead from the appearances of the things which we see with our eyes to the first causes of their being in growth, although this may be of no immediate practical use to us. The other creatures and the human body are kept alive by taking food and drink. But the human soul is something quite different from the other parts of the human, and the soul is kept alive, enriched, and grows by the food called knowledge.[10]

Gregory of Nyssa says that God is the food of the soul.[11] For Kepler, science provided this food. For him the nourishment comes not in perceiving the created world with the senses but in the mind penetrating deeper through scientific theorizing to understand the patterns of God's creative activity. It may be that for Kepler scientific discovery became itself a kind of contemplation, a way of looking intensely through the moving stars

8. Translated in Frankenberry, *Faith of Scientists*, 44, alt.
9. In German, "mind" and "spirit" are the same word, *Geist*.
10. Translated in Frankenberry, *Faith of Scientists*, 44, alt.
11. *On Infants' Early Deaths*; trans. Moore and Wilson, *Gregory*, 375–76.

and planets to trace the presence and work of their Creator in them. In the twentieth century, as we shall see, Einstein speaks of a similar kind of contemplation, though like Kepler, he does not name it as such. Such contemplation fulfills the purpose of God's image, drawing the human person to God.

Einstein, a Disguised Theologian

Albert Einstein (1879–1955) is of course known as the greatest physicist of the twentieth century and was widely perceived as a genius in his own lifetime. Because of this, people asked him questions about all kinds of things, including religion, and he often wrote answers to their questions. He was Jewish but not observant. Yet, as the Swiss novelist Friedrich Dürrenmatt observed, he "used to speak so often of God that I tend to believe he has been a disguised theologian."[12] He was genuinely awed and fascinated by the God he found through his study of the physical world's structures.

Einstein's work as a theoretical physicist sought to show how different kinds of matter and energy—from subatomic particles, through the objects in our everyday world, to the planets and stars—all follow the same mathematical laws. He demonstrated the interdependence of the three dimensions of space and a fourth dimension, time, so he was the first to envision the universe as a single space-time continuum. Though he never attained this goal, he aimed to discover how the four forces in nature, that is, electromagnetism, gravity, and the strong and weak forces that join subatomic particles, are all interconnected, something that would be described in a "unified field theory." As Nancy Frankenberry says, "His life-long compulsion to unify . . . was especially apparent in his religious sense of the universe."[13]

His awareness of God, like Kepler's, came directly from his scientific work. Einstein writes, "My comprehension of God comes

---

12. Frankenberry, *Faith of Scientists*, 143.
13. Frankenberry, *Faith of Scientists*, 144; see also 146–47.

from the deeply felt conviction of a superior intelligence that reveals itself in the knowable world." In perceiving how physical reality is put together, he traces the threads woven by the Creator. He cannot believe that his own mind invented the beautiful and detailed ways he finds things interconnected, and he describes his experience as follows: "In every true searcher of Nature there is a kind of religious reverence, for he finds it impossible to imagine that he is the first to have thought out the exceedingly delicate threads that connect his perceptions."[14] Like Kepler, with his human mind he follows the creative activities of the divine mind, though he does not speak explicitly of the image of God.

Elsewhere, Einstein describes his experience of God through scientific discovery as "cosmic religious feeling." He turns his attention away from petty personal concerns to the vastness, magnificence, and unity of the universe. He describes his experience as follows: "The individual feels the futility of human desires and aims and the sublimity and marvelous order which reveal themselves both in nature and in the world of thought. Individual existence impresses him as a sort of prison and he wants to experience the universe as a single significant whole."[15] In a different place, he explains the same experience in another way, showing how it arises from his work of finding equations that describe the universe's order and unity. He senses "admiration for the beauty and belief in the logical simplicity of the order and harmony that we can grasp humbly and only imperfectly."[16] The creation's vastness teaches him humility by showing him how little he understands. He discovered more than did the physicists who came before him, yet he knew his knowledge was small compared to the whole cosmos.

Einstein's turn away from personal concerns and toward God's creation is at the core of his approach to life. Like the mindset of the desert fathers and mothers, his attitude to life was ascetical and devotional. To be sure, he was married, and

14. Quoted in Frankenberry, *Faith of Scientists*, 151.
15. Einstein, *On Religion and Science*, quoted in Frankenberry, *Faith of Scientists*, 155.
16. Frankenberry, *Faith of Scientists*, 152; see also 163–64.

his wife did a great deal to support him in his work and enable him to manage the demands his fame placed on him.[17] Yet he sums up his attitude in the following paragraph, in which one senses the call of the desert:

How strange is the lot of us mortals! Each of us is here for a brief sojourn; for what purpose he knows not, though he sometimes thinks he senses it. But without deeper reflection one knows from daily life that one exists for other people—first of all for those upon whose smiles and well being our own happiness is wholly dependent, and then for the many, unknown to us, to whose destinies we are bound by the ties of sympathy. A hundred times every day I remind myself that my inner and outer life are based on the labors of other people, living and dead, and that I must exert myself in order to give in the same measure as I have received and am still receiving. I am strongly drawn to a frugal life and am often oppressively aware that I am consuming an undue amount of the labor of my fellow humans. I regard class distinctions as unjustified and, in the last resort, based on force. I also believe that a simple and unassuming life is good for everybody, physically and mentally.[18]

His frugality, simplicity of life, and sense of justice toward his neighbors are the marks of an ascetic lifestyle. He is mindful of his connectedness with others and his indebtedness to them, so like the early desert monks he reminds himself of these facts repeatedly and strives to base his conduct on them. Like his scientific work, these attitudes toward others strengthen his humility.

Einstein recognizes that faith and devotion are what make scientific work possible. This is particularly true of theoretical science, like his work in physics. His work did not yield immediate useful results, such as new technology or medical techniques, so how does he remain motivated to do it? Einstein says that

17. See Antonina Vallentin, *The Drama of Albert Einstein* (Garden City, NY: Doubleday, 1954).

18. Albert Einstein, "The World as I See It," in *Ideas and Opinions*, trans. Sonja Bargmann (New York: Bonanza Books, 1954), 8.

what motivates him to pursue long and laborious research is his awareness of God. He writes, "Science can only be created by those who are thoroughly imbued with the aspiration toward truth and understanding. This source of feeling, however, springs from the sphere of religion." He adds that scientists also need faith in the rationality of phenomena in the world and faith in the capacity of human reason to comprehend them.[19] That is, they need to have confidence that the world has a coherent structure and is not a disorderly mess, that they can hope to discern the world's structure by using their reason, and that the same experiments done in the same ways will continue to yield the same results. Truth and order in the universe come from God, and so does human understanding. The fact that there is a link between the structure of the universe and the human mind is itself a cause of wonder; it is a link between God and God's image, and it makes science possible.

The aspiration toward truth, as Einstein recognizes, is a longing for God. This longing is what sustains the researcher's efforts. Einstein makes the same point at greater length elsewhere, again naming the experience of God as "cosmic religious feeling." In this passage, notice how he speaks of his predecessors, whose struggles he can understand from his own experience:

> The cosmic religious feeling is the strongest and noblest motive for scientific research. Only those who realize the immense efforts and, above all, the devotion without which pioneer work in theoretical science cannot be achieved are able to grasp the strength of the emotion out of which alone such work, remote as it is from the immediate realities of life, can issue. What a deep conviction of the rationality of the universe and what a yearning to understand . . . Kepler and Newton must have had to enable them to spend years of solitary labor in disentangling the principles of celestial mechanics! Those whose acquaintance with scientific research is derived chiefly from its practical results easily develop a completely false notion of the mentality of the people who, surrounded

19. Frankenberry, *Faith of Scientists*, 161.

by a skeptical world, have shown the way to kindred spirits scattered wide through the world and through the centuries. Only one who has devoted his life to similar ends can have a vivid realization of what has inspired these people and given them the strength to remain true to their purpose in spite of countless failures. It is cosmic religious feeling that gives a person such strength.[20]

When he developed his new theories, Einstein concentrated deeply on the physical data and the mathematics he used to describe them. Through his intense use of reason (*ratio, dianoia*), his spiritual intellect (*intellectus, nous*)[21] must have become engaged. Through gazing intently at the order of the created world, he perceived the presence of the Creator who gave it order. This experience resulted in the "cosmic religious feeling" that sustained his work and evoked his awe, wonder, admiration, and amazement.

A truly religious attitude combines wonder and incomprehension, since the divine is both revealed to creation and concealed from it. Einstein and other great scientists share both of these attitudes. For example, his predecessor in physics, Isaac Newton (1643–1727), compared his research to a child's play: "I do not know what I may appear to the world, but to myself I seem to have been only like a boy playing on the seashore, and diverting myself in now and then finding a smoother pebble or a prettier shell than ordinary, whilst the great ocean of truth lay all undiscovered before me."[22] Einstein too compared himself to a child:

We are in the position of a little child entering a huge library filled with books in many languages. The child knows someone must have written those books. It does not know how. It does not understand the languages in which they are written. The child dimly suspects a mysterious order in the arrangement of the

20. *On Religion and Science*; quoted in Frankenberry, *Faith of Scientists*, 157, alt.

21. For this distinction between scientific reason and spiritual intellect, see chapter 3, above.

22. Frankenberry, *Faith of Scientists*, 107.

books but doesn't know what it is. That, it seems to me, is the
attitude of even the most intelligent human being toward God.
We see the universe marvelously arranged and obeying certain
laws but only dimly understand those laws. Our limited minds
grasp the mysterious force that moves the constellations.[23]

Like a young reader who does not know the book's author,
Einstein acknowledges that he can dimly grasp the patterns of
God's work but cannot perceive God directly.

Einstein, who first used mathematics to envision the universe
as four dimensions, understood that he and others could not
picture what this would look like. He again speaks of God's
incomprehensibility using the standard theological metaphor
of a clock and a clockmaker, but then switches to a metaphor
extrapolating from his own physics: "I see a pattern, but my
imagination cannot picture the maker of that pattern. I see a
clock, but I cannot envision the clockmaker. The human mind
is unable to conceive of four dimensions, so how can it conceive of a God, before whom a thousand years and a thousand
dimensions are as one?"[24]

The incomprehensibility of God grounds the incomprehen-
sible vastness of the universe. It ensures that there is always
more for scientists to investigate and discover. So the scientist's
spirituality is characterized by wonder and incomprehension,
which in turn fuel intense longing for more knowledge. "The
important thing is not to stop questioning," Einstein says. "Curiosity has its own reason for existence. One cannot help but
be in awe when [one] contemplates the mysteries of eternity,
of life, of the marvelous structure of reality. It is enough if one
tries merely to comprehend a little of this mystery each day.
Never lose a holy curiosity."[25] This curiosity is holy because it
is a longing for God, as Einstein explains elsewhere: "I want to
know how God created this world. I am not interested in this

23. Frankenberry, *Faith of Scientists*, 153.
24. Frankenberry, *Faith of Scientists*, 152.
25. Quoted in Ronald W. Clark, *Einstein: The Life and Times* (New York: World,
1971), 622.

or that phenomenon, in the spectrum of this or that element. I want to know his thoughts. The rest are details."[26]

Science, Art, and the Image of God

We have seen that Kepler compared the painter and the musician to the astronomer who finds joy in the wonder of the skies. Einstein made a similar comparison between science and art, and he found the root of both in the divine mystery: "The most beautiful thing we can experience is the mysterious. It is the source of all true art and science. He to whom this emotion is a stranger, who can no longer pause to wonder and stand rapt in awe, is as good as dead: his eyes are closed. This insight into the mystery of life . . . has also given rise to religion."[27] For Einstein, the perception of beauty that elicits wonder is what makes life worth living. To put it another way, this perception and this response are what make life truly human. They manifest the image of God.

Scientists often study the world to find ways of serving creation or their neighbors. We saw in the last chapter how scientific work has been necessary to save the California condors from extinction. Theoretical science, which we have considered in this chapter, often yields unforeseen practical benefits, but these usually come long after the initial discoveries, sometimes generations later. The theoretical scientists themselves, like Kepler and Einstein, are simply searching for more knowledge of the world in which they live. They examine the natural world, often using scientific instruments and experiments to see farther and more clearly than they could with their senses alone. They analyze what they have seen, and then they share their new knowledge with others. Their tasks are perception, rational analysis, and sharing in the human community. All of these activities are manifestations of the divine image.

The painter, too, looks at the world, or at people, and the musician listens. They perceive something there that others have

26. Frankenberry, *Faith of Scientists*, 152.
27. Frankenberry, *Faith of Scientists*, 154.

not perceived. Then they use their gifts and disciplined training to express what they perceive and to share it with others. Thus the arts and sciences both enact a relationship between the created world and the human community, a relationship of receiving and sharing insight and wonder.

Nancy Zamboni, a Christian woman I knew in college, majored in religious studies but has become an artist and art teacher. She paints still lifes, trees, and flowers blooming in the garden, ordinary things that seem to smile in her pictures. She told me she paints in order to show people the beauty they would otherwise not notice. A particular interest for her has been to paint light shining through windows. This light's translucency is an everyday occurrence but reveals a glimpse of God's glory. She often saw images of beauty but could not paint them all. Then she took up photography. She takes a camera with her as she goes out, and when she sees something that attracts her artist's eye, she takes a photograph so she can preserve and share what she has seen.

The Icon and God's Image and Likeness

Sometimes, as with Kepler and Einstein, the artist's perception of created realities deepens into a contemplation of God. This is particularly true of the icons found in the Orthodox Church, though they are different from other kinds of visual art and have a distinctive purpose. The word "icon" is actually a transliteration of the Greek word translated "image," as in "image of God." This means that the Son, Jesus Christ, is the perfect image, or icon, of God the Father, like him in everything except that he is the Son and not himself the Father. And though not completely like God, the human being is created as an image, or icon, of God. After we have fallen, it is God who restores his image and repaints his likeness in us.[28] By practicing virtues,

---

28. Athanasius, *On the Incarnation* 14.1–2; ed. Cross, *Athanasius*, 21–22, discussed in chapter 2, above.

we are also called to craft God's likeness in ourselves.[29] In this work of creation and restoration, God is the first iconographer, and we humans are also called to be iconographers as we work to make ourselves into likenesses of God's virtues. The task of an iconographer painting a wooden panel should be seen in this context, as a particular vocation that echoes what is universally human. Likewise, if people who look at icons see in them the presence of God or an anticipation of the kingdom to come, they are also called to discern God and his kingdom in their neighbors as they strive to welcome God within themselves.

Art generally, like Zamboni's still lifes and landscapes, aims to reveal the beauty of things in this world. The icons, by contrast, aim to reveal what will only be fully manifest in God's future. The eighth-century theologian John of Damascus says that because God became incarnate as Jesus Christ, he lived and was seen by others in a human body. Because people around him saw his body and his face, his humanity can be depicted in an icon, although God as such remains invisible. Since Christ is both divine and human, his image reveals the perfect actualization of the divine image in his humanity, and it also reveals God present in Christ's flesh. Saints can also be depicted in icons, which show people in whom God dwells and who have attained God's likeness. The icons of Christ and the saints also show the life of the resurrection, of the kingdom to come.[30] To portray the age to come, icons show the divine glory as light shining forth from *within* people and things, illuminating everything. This glory is markedly different from, and greater than, the radiance of sunlight shining on the outward surfaces of things and casting shadows behind them.

In the eighth and ninth centuries, there was a dispute in the Byzantine Church about whether there should be icons. John of Damascus argued in favor of icons and in the process explained their meaning and purpose. He saw a parallel between

---

29. Gregory of Nyssa, *On Perfection*; trans. Callahan, *Gregory of Nyssa*, 110, discussed in chapter 4, above.

30. Leonid Ouspensky, *Theology of the Icon*, trans. Anthony Gythiel and Elizabeth Theokritoff, 2 vols. (Crestwood, NY: St. Vladimir's Seminary Press, 1992), 1:151–94.

the words of Scripture and what is depicted in an icon: "Everywhere we use our senses to produce an image of the Incarnate God himself, and we sanctify . . . sight . . . , just as by words hearing is sanctified. . . . The word appeals to hearing, the image appeals to sight; it conveys understanding."[31] Thus the word and the image disclose the same reality. So people can perceive the kingdom of God in the depths of either the biblical text or the icon's mosaic and painted wood. To maintain this parallel faithfully, the Orthodox Church has strict rules for how icons are to be made and what is to be depicted in them, just as it has rules for theological writing. Icons are supposed to depict what is found in Scripture. For example, at the baptism of Christ, the Holy Spirit is portrayed as a dove, but the dove is not a picture of the Spirit in other contexts. So in the icon of Pentecost, the Spirit appears as tongues of fire.

John of Damascus quotes Basil of Caesarea, who compares word and image:

> Both writers of words and painters many times describe clearly human deeds of valor in war, the first adorning them with rhetoric [i.e., elaborate literary language], the second inscribing them on tablets, and both arousing many to deeds of excellence. For what the word of a story makes present through hearing, the very same is shown silently in a picture.[32]

Here Basil speaks of how tales of warriors in ancient literature could inspire courage and perseverance in people who heard them. In quoting this passage, John is thinking of beholding the icons of martyrs and other saints, people who bear God's likeness, and then being inspired to follow their example by striving for virtue and thereby attaining God's likeness too. John's point is that icons can provide such inspiration, just as narratives can.

Those who behold icons can find the same inspiration in our own time. Pavel Florensky (1882–1937) was a twentieth-century

---

31. *On the Divine Images* 1.17; trans. Louth, *John of Damascus*, 31.
32. *On the Divine Images* 1.46; trans. Louth, *John of Damascus*, 45–46.

Russian Orthodox priest, mathematician, chemist, and theologian who himself became a martyr under the Communist
regime. In language that uses contemporary psychological concepts, he writes of his experiences looking at icons:

> An icon recalls its prototype. Thus, in one beholder, it will awaken
> in the bright clarities of his conscious mind a spiritual vision that
> matches the bright clarities of the icon; and the beholder's vision
> will be completely clear and conscious. But in another person,
> the icon will stir the dreams that lie deeper in the subconscious,
> awakening a perception of the spiritual that not only affirms
> that such seeing is possible but also brings the thing seen into
> immediately felt experience. Thus, at the highest flourishing of
> their prayer, the ancient ascetics found that their icons were not
> simply windows through which they could behold the holy faces
> depicted on them but were also doorways through which their
> faces actually entered the empirical world. The saints came down
> from the icons to appear before those praying to them.[33]

In this passage, Florensky is speaking not of prayer to God
but of face-to-face conversation between the ascetic, perhaps
one of the desert fathers or mothers we have discussed in this
book, and the saint depicted in an icon. Christ, who is risen
and has overcome death, brings the departed saint and the living ascetic together, for they are both members of his mystical
body.

Icons are painted in reverse perspective. That is, things do not
appear smaller in the background to show their distance from
the viewer. Instead, they appear larger.[34] So the icon portrays a
different kind of space from the ordinary, a space that draws the
viewer into silent conversation with the persons depicted. Again
speaking from his own experience, Florensky describes how the
space within the icon overpowers the beholder's space:

33. Pavel Florensky, *Iconostasis*, trans. Donald Sheehan and Olga Andrejev (Crestwood, NY: St. Vladimir's Seminary Press, 1996), 71–72, alt.

34. A good example is Andrei Rublev's famous icon of the Holy Trinity. There is
a reproduction at www.calvin.edu/worship/stories/images/trinitarian_worship.php
(accessed April 2, 2009). For reverse perspective, look at the footstools.

Like light pouring forth light, the icon stands revealed. And no matter where the icon is physically located in the space where we encounter it, we can only describe our experience of seeing it as *a beholding that ascends.* Our seeing rises above everything around us, for we recognize that we are, in this act of seeing, existing in the icon's space in eternity. In such acts of seeing, the fires of our lusts and the emptiness of our earthly hungers simply and wholly cease; and we recognize the vision as something that, in essence, exceeds the empirical world, as something acting upon us *from its own dominion.* . . . We testify to the icon's triumphant beauty overwhelming everything.[35]

Clearly, Florensky's experiences are extraordinary, though many Orthodox Christians can identify with at least a little of what he so eloquently describes. Beholding an icon, standing in front of it in prayer for a period of time, can indeed have the effect of calming temptations, as he indicates. Through looking at the icon of a saint who bears the divine likeness, people can gradually and imperceptibly become more like God.

The Iconographer and the Image of God

It is difficult to portray the realities of the age to come or of the spiritual realm that already participates in it. These realities are known to the church as a community and especially to those persons who are closest to Christ. Iconographers are not supposed to paint what they see in their own imagination, nor are they to paint from a living model, as if a man posing in the studio were a replica of St. Peter or even of Christ. Instead, iconographers copy older icons. The icons they copy are known as authentic because when faithful people pray in front of them, they serve as windows, or doors, into the kingdom of God.

Yet how can a person become an iconographer? The obvious way is to study under one who is experienced in this sacred art. But one of the greatest icon painters and teachers of iconography in the twentieth century, Leonid Ouspensky (1902–1987),

---

35. Florensky, *Iconostasis*, 72, emphasis in the original.

became interested in icons as a refugee in Paris. Under the circumstances, he had no master iconographer to teach him. He learned by studying old icons.

Ouspensky, the son of a Russian landowner, did not believe in God as he was growing up. When he was a young man, the country was torn apart by the civil war that led to the Communist revolution. He joined the Red Army and barely escaped death several times. Then he was captured by the opposing army and put to work. After a while he fled into Europe and made his way to Paris, where many Russian refugees would settle. He did various jobs along the way, always working with his hands. He ended up at a bicycle factory, and though he was poor he began taking art classes.

One of his fellow students challenged him to paint an icon, and he said that of course he could. When he tried to do so, he found it very difficult. After he finished his first attempt at an icon, "he destroyed it, realizing that he had done something inappropriate."[36] Yet he gradually became more interested in icons, and through this interest he came to an authentic faith in Christ and returned to the Russian Orthodox Church. At that time there were numerous icons in the antique shops of Paris. He could not afford to buy them, so he spent many hours in the shops studying them. He later said that the old icons were his best teachers. Subsequently, besides creating superb icons, he studied and taught the history of Orthodox iconography and wrote books about it. He also taught icon painting and thereby trained many other iconographers.[37]

In the Russian church, there are long-standing rules about iconographers. They must be trained by other iconographers, and their work must be certified by bishops before the church can accept it.[38] In the refugee community in Paris, Ouspensky

36. See his wife's account of his life in Lydia Ouspensky, "A Short Biography: Leonid Alexandrovich Ouspensky," in Patrick Doolan, *Recovering the Icon: The Life and Work of Leonid Ouspensky* (Crestwood, NY: St. Vladimir's Seminary Press, 2006), 12. This lovely book contains reproductions of many of Ouspensky's icons.

37. Ouspensky, "A Short Biography," 11–14.

38. Florensky, *Iconostasis*, 90–95.

did not have access to any of this guidance. Yet he also prayed a great deal, especially when working in his studio, and he lived a disciplined spiritual life, as is traditional for iconographers. These practices enabled him to be in contact with God's kingdom, which he was called to depict. But Ouspensky had to discover through his own studies and the work of his own hands how to paint icons. Perhaps as a result, his icons are very traditional yet look new and fresh. They clearly reflect the twentieth century in which he lived.

"To paint icons as they were painted by the ancient and holy iconographers meant to follow tradition," Ouspensky says. And yet, he adds, "It is not a matter of copying the ancient iconographers."[39] Patrick Doolan, a student of iconography, started by tracing old icons in order to make new ones that would look the same. When he went to study with Ouspensky, the teacher immediately told him not to do this. Instead, he had to learn to draw icons, imitating the original by eye rather than using tracing paper. These drawings would become patterns for the new icons.[40] This procedure also has enough flexibility to allow the painter to make subtle but significant alterations in the design. As Ouspensky explains:

> Iconography therefore is not copying. It is far from being impersonal, for to follow tradition never shackles the creative powers of the iconographer, whose individuality expresses itself in the composition as well as in color and line. . . . The absence of identical icons has been noted long ago. Indeed, among icons on the same subject, although they are sometimes remarkably alike, we never find two identical icons (except in cases of deliberate copying in more modern times). Icons are not *copied*, but are *painted from*, which means their free creative transposition.[41]

Ouspensky notes elsewhere that the iconographer works as a member of the community, the body of Christ.[42] His or her task

39. Ouspensky, *Theology of the Icon*, 1:11.
40. Doolan, *Recovering the Icon*, 95–96.
41. Quoted in Doolan, *Recovering the Icon*, 96, emphasis in the original.
42. Ouspensky, *Theology of the Icon*, 1:11.

is to portray the whole community's shared perception of the kingdom of God. And yet each iconographer, and ideally each icon, is unique. This combination of community and individual uniqueness is characteristic of humankind as created in the image of the Holy Trinity. We will discuss this point further in the next chapter.

As Ouspensky says, "Being an expression of the image and likeness of God restored in [humankind], the icon is a dynamic and constructive element of worship." It is dynamic because it points the way to our goal as human beings: "Icons are like markers on our path to the new creation." Thus the icon is an answer to human questions, "a teaching and a guide, . . . a task to accomplish, . . . a prefiguration and the first fruits of the Kingdom of God."[43] It presents to people the task of drawing close to Christ, overcoming sin, practicing virtue, and thus becoming themselves God's likeness. The iconographer must pursue this goal in order to portray it with clarity and truth in painting or mosaic. The beholder is challenged to imitate Christ and the saints and thus to participate in the world disclosed in the icon.

Conclusion

Einstein lived a life of perseverance, humility, service to others, wonder, awareness of mystery, and holy curiosity about the universe God created. His disciplined spiritual life enabled him to discover with his human mind the thoughts in the Creator's mind. Ouspensky too lived a disciplined life of prayer and simplicity, following the practices of his church. This enabled him through his painter's eyes and hands to disclose to his contemporaries in the twentieth century the radiance of the saints. One found God through his scientific research, the other through his artistic work. Both used the skills of human culture to build bridges from the ordinary circumstances of the present life to the kingdom of God. They, together with Johannes Kepler,

43. Ouspensky, *Theology of the Icon*, 1:192–93.

Nancy Zamboni, and countless others, have shown how the arts and sciences can enable people to find God. And as they have found their way, their works communicate that path to others. So they show that there is a connection between human culture and God's kingdom, which is the goal of our creation in the divine image. Artistic perception and scientific reason, when used rightly, are themselves aligned to the spiritual intellect, which is the focal point of the divine image within the human person. Then these different kinds of mental functioning can all come to manifest the image of God.

And yet, as we have seen throughout this book, fallen human beings can use the gifts of the divine image to turn away from God, harm each other, and damage the created world. The arts and sciences give human communities great power to create their own imaginary worlds and then immerse themselves in them, forgetting that God even exists. So we need to make choices in how we will use these powers and what our goals will be. Ultimately, only God has the wisdom and the stability to create and sustain a harmonious, life-giving, and just world. Our task is to cooperate with him.

9

Community

We live in a time of fragmentation. People of different genders, classes, ethnicities, races, and cultures are often thought to live in different worlds so that only women can understand women, only Chinese can understand Chinese, and so on. This is surely true to some extent. But why, then, can Jane Austen compellingly portray men as well as women in her novels? Why can men as well as women understand them? And why are people today still interested in reading them even though they were written in a different century, a different country, and a different culture? Novels are written about specific characters in particular contexts. Yet surely the reason why world literature remains interesting to readers today is that there are important things all people share as human beings. Great literature plumbs the depths of themes that are universal.

The image of God is universally human. So the facets of the divine image we have discussed in this book are things that all people share: freedom to choose, closeness to God and Christ, perception of spiritual realities, capacity for virtues, royal dignity, embodiment, ability to care for the created world, and the capacity to create and communicate arts and sciences. A person may have more of some of these gifts and less of others, but ultimately they are all characteristically human. These shared characteristics bring people together so they can walk side by side toward the same ultimate goals.

And yet in human communities, people are not only alike but also different. So how can people who differ still interact positively with each other? How do they give and take? How are they made one while each remains unique? Can their uniqueness itself strengthen their unity? Finally, how does the community formed among diverse people manifest the divine image?

In Genesis 1:26, God says, "Let us make humankind in our image, according to our likeness" (NRSV). God is speaking in the plural: "Let *us* make." And the God in whose image and likeness humans are made is also named as a plural; it is "*our* image" and "*our* likeness." But the *making* is a single action. Early Christians, such as Basil of Caesarea, saw in these words a reference to the Holy Trinity. That is, the Father, the Son, and the Holy Spirit deliberate together and decide to make humankind. And as they create the human, they act together as one God.[1] And yet the image that is imprinted into the human is the image of the three together, the Holy Trinity.

How, then, can humankind become a likeness of the Trinity? This question is of great interest today. Theologians from many different Christian traditions agree that humans bear the Trinity's likeness when they live together harmoniously as a community. Christians in the fourth century were thinking through both the theology of the divine image and the theology of the Trinity. At that time they only provided hints of how the two doctrines come together. Yet they did, in different ways, begin to connect human community, the divine image, and the Trinity. Their suggestions indicate a direction that today's theologians can follow.

1. Basil, *On the Origin of Humanity* 1.3–4; trans. Harrison, *St. Basil*, 33–34.

Gregory of Nazianzus and a Church in Conflict

The three Cappadocian theologians lived when trinitarian questions were a major issue in the church, and they all reflected on the Trinity. Yet the one who probably thought most deeply and most creatively about how God is Trinity was Gregory of Nazianzus. As a pastor responsible for helping congregations live together as Christians, he was concerned about how people maintain peaceful communities. As he struggled in a world full of conflicts, he made the connection between the Holy Trinity and its image in human communal life. He believed that just as we each have the task of acquiring and practicing virtues that are like God's virtues,[2] it is also our task to live together after the pattern of the three divine persons, that is, lovingly, harmoniously, with sharing and mutual respect.

Gregory's father was the bishop, that is, the chief pastor, in Nazianzus, a small town in Cappadocia. His name was also Gregory, and to distinguish him from his famous son he is known as Gregory the Elder. After his young son Gregory had returned home from the brilliant life of a college town, his father ordained him to the priesthood. The son was unhappy with this decision because he wanted to devote his life to prayer, study, and writing, not to being a pastor. He ran away for a few months to Basil's monastery but then returned, willing to serve. Soon the congregation needed his unique gifts.

He was called to heal a schism in the local community. It seems that Gregory the Elder, who was not trained as a theologian, made an imprecise statement about the Trinity. By doing so, he stumbled in the great controversy of the time. Some monks in the local area broke with him and withdrew from the congregation. The younger Gregory, as it happened, had ties to people on both sides. He was close to his family, but he also lived as a monk and so was close to the monks who had left. He talked to members of both groups and persuaded each side to make concessions. When the monks came back to his father's church,

2. See chapter 4, above.

the younger Gregory preached the homily that cemented, ratified, and celebrated their reunion. Fortunately, this homily has come down to us. The young preacher was devoted to God as Trinity and went on to become one of the great trinitarian theologians of all time.

In the resolution of this early pastoral crisis, Gregory speaks of his people's rediscovered unity as an image of the Holy Trinity. "Now," he says, "belonging to the One we have become one, and belonging to the Trinity we have come to be the same in nature and in soul and in honor."[3] That is, the congregation's newfound unity is an image of God's oneness. Yet the people do not merge into one thing, like lumps of clay that a potter piles together into a single lump; they remain distinct persons. Their distinctness, in fact, is also an image of the Trinity, which remains three, though it is one. Moreover, as Gregory affirms, the three divine persons always remain alike in their nature— that is, in what they are—and equal in honor and dignity. So he proclaims that the members of his congregation, by coming to an agreement, have reaffirmed that in their Christian faith they are alike. By overcoming conflict and honoring one another, they have also affirmed that all are equal in dignity. So as the conflict is ended, they not only believe in the Trinity, they *act* as its image and likeness.

In this sermon, Gregory goes on to offer the angels as an example for his congregation to follow as they work to preserve their peace and mutual love. The angels, he says,

> remain in their own condition, which first is peace and absence of division, having received unity as a gift of the Holy Trinity, from which also comes their illumination. For it is one God and is believed to be such, no less because of its harmony than because of its sameness of essence. So those [people] belong to God and are close to divine realities who are shown as embracing the good of peace and rejecting the opposite, division.[4]

3. *Oration* 6.4; ed. Calvet-Sebasti, *Grégoire de Nazianze*, 130.
4. *Oration* 6.13; ed. Calvet-Sebasti, *Grégoire de Nazianze*, 154–56.

The harmony named here characterizes the Trinity as community of persons, while the sameness of essence characterizes God as one. Gregory goes on to hint that peace in a human community is the image and likeness of God, thereby identifying the human as an image of the Trinity. He adds a further exhortation that makes this point explicitly:

> Only one thing can constrain us to such benevolence and harmony, the imitation of God and of divine realities. Toward this alone it is prudent for the soul to look, having come into being according to the image of God, that it may preserve its nobility as far as possible through inclination toward the divine and, to the extent it is able, likeness to it.[5]

Here the divine perfection members of the congregation are invited to share is harmony, whose model within God can only be the communal life of the Trinity.

The Unity of Humankind

The unity of humankind is an important facet of the image of God, who is one. Humankind is a multiplicity of persons who are united in one body, just as God is three persons united in one essence. In an important passage, Gregory of Nazianzus's friend Gregory of Nyssa locates the divine image not in one human individual, or even many individuals considered separately, but in humankind as a whole.

> As a particular human being is enclosed by the size of his body, . . . so, it seems to me, the whole fullness of humanity was encompassed by the God of all through the power of foreknowledge, as if in one body. And the text teaches this which says, "And God created the human . . . , in the image of God he created him" [Gen. 1:27 RSV, alt.]. For the image is not in part of

5. *Oration* 6.14; ed. Calvet-Sebasti, *Grégoire de Nazianze*, 156.

[human] nature, . . . but such power extends equally to all the [human] race.[6]

In Genesis 1:26, the RSV translates the word I have rendered as "the human" as "man," which is singular. The NRSV has "humankind" and "he created them," which would support Gregory's interpretation more than would the Greek Septuagint he must have read. To translate *adam* (Hebrew) or *anthrōpos* (Greek) as "humankind" in this context would beg the question he is addressing. Adam in Genesis functions as both an individual character in the story and a representative who sums up all of humanity. In a way, Adam is both singular and plural. Gregory may have sensed this ambivalence when he chose to cite Genesis 1:26 in this passage, because he is saying that the one man Adam signifies all humankind.

Gregory borrows from Paul the metaphor of humankind as a body (see 1 Cor. 12:12). Gregory says that a human body occupies a definite, measurable amount of space. Similarly, humankind as a whole includes a finite number of people. So Gregory envisions God, who is infinite, as embracing in his foreknowledge and his power the whole human race, which, however large it is, is still finite. God's power creates and sustains the divine image in humans, and he can easily reach all of them at once. So Gregory understands the human being mentioned in Genesis 1:26–27 to mean the totality of all human beings considered together.

Gregory then says that all humans possess rationality and the other facets of the divine image, which shows that the image extends to all people. He adds that the same divine image is found throughout human history, from the initial creation to the eschaton. This is because God encompasses all of time, just as he encompasses all of space:

The human being manifested at the first creation of the world and the one that will come into being at the [final] consumma-

6. *On the Creation of Humanity* 16.17; PG 44.185B–C; trans. Moore and Wilson, *Gregory*, 406, alt.

tion of all are alike, equally bearing in themselves the divine image. Because of this, the whole [of humankind] was named [in Gen. 1:27] as one human being, since to the power of God nothing is either past or future, but what will be is encompassed equally with what is present by the energy that rules all. So the whole nature, extending from the first to the last, is, as it were, one image of the Existing One.[7]

Gregory's point is that humankind is a unity in which all humans are ultimately alike. He does, however, acknowledge diversity here and now. Yet he believes that at the eschaton everybody will have attained to the full stature of Christ, so then all will be Christlike, that is, all will be alike. In the meantime, because we each manifest different facets of Christ's likeness but not the whole of it, we remain different.

Diversity in Unity

Yet the Trinity is Father, Son, and Holy Spirit, who differ in their relationships to one another. Moreover, as Vladimir Lossky, a twentieth-century Orthodox theologian, says, just as God's unity of being is an unfathomable mystery, so also each of the three divine persons is unique in an unfathomably mysterious way.[8] So, cannot human diversity, the mysterious and irreducible uniqueness of each person, serve as an image of the Trinity's diversity, even when people have attained the fullness of God's likeness? In other words, cannot human diversity be included in the divine image and likeness? Does it not have intrinsic reality and value?

To find an understanding of the ultimate reality and value of diversity among humans, it is best to look to others besides Gregory of Nyssa, maybe to today's theologians. Historians of ideas have found that modern people understand personal

7. *On the Creation of Humanity* 16.17–18; PG 44:185C–D; trans. Moore and Wilson, *Gregory*, 406, alt.

8. Vladimir Lossky, *The Mystical Theology of the Eastern Church* (Cambridge and London: James Clarke, 1957), 54.

uniqueness more clearly than did those in ancient times. Yet such a study goes beyond the scope of this book. There are, however, insights in early Christian writers such as John Chrysostom, who wrote about family life, and Gregory's brother Basil, who wrote about monastic community. Let us consider what they say about community and diversity.

In a family, mother, father, and children differ from one another, yet they are united as each makes a unique contribution to the life they share. Each family, in fact, is made up of people with unique gifts, and they live together in unique circumstances. They collaborate in various ways to provide the things each one needs. For example, I recently heard about a family in which the father lost his job due to the 2009 recession. He stays home and cares for the children because his wife is a physician and works long hours. She is supporting the family financially as she cares for the sick. John Chrysostom believed that family life can be an image of the Trinity. He says that in their life together, husband and wife, who are united through their difference from each other, are an image of the Father and the Son.[9]

Chrysostom's explanation of how God created humans united and alike is less abstract than Gregory of Nyssa's explanation, discussed above. It is based on Genesis 2. He compares humankind to a tree with many branches that grows from Adam, who is its root. Eve comes next, since she was created from the side of Adam, and then come their offspring, for she is the "mother of all living" (Gen. 3:20).

> [God] permitted Adam to marry Eve, who was more than sister or daughter, she was his own flesh! God caused the entire human race to proceed from this one point of origin. He did not, on the one hand, fashion woman independently from man; otherwise man would think of her as essentially different from himself. Nor did he enable woman to bear children without man; if this were the case she would be self-sufficient. Instead, just as the branches of a tree proceed from a single trunk, he made the one man Adam to be the origin of all humankind, both male

9. *Homily 20 on Ephesians* 4; PG 62:140.

and female, and made it impossible for men and women to be self-sufficient.[10]

According to Chrysostom, who interprets Genesis literally, the one man Adam, the root of humankind, guarantees the alikeness and the unity of the whole. In other words, if God had created Adam from the earth and then created Eve from the earth, as he created the other animals, she would be a different species from her husband-to-be. So God ensures that humans all have the same human nature—that is, in terms of modern biology, they are all the same species—by creating her from Adam. After the first couple, men and women are dependent on each other for their births, that is, for their very existence. All boys have mothers, and all girls have fathers. This shows how fundamental the interdependence of family members really is. This means that men and women are united as the same species but are different in ways that enable them to collaborate in procreation and in other aspects of life. They can share with one another in many ways, since each has gifts the other lacks. The family's unity is built on their alikeness, but it is also built on their diversity.

According to the story in Genesis 2, the distinction between male and female is the first kind of human diversity, and the family is the first kind of human community. During subsequent history, many other kinds of diversity have arisen too, and with them many kinds of community. Differences of race, class, culture, ethnicity, and personality, among others, give people different gifts they can share and exchange with one another. These differences enable each person to appreciate others who are different from the self, to learn from them, and to value them. For example, Westerners can build boats that run on gasoline and navigate using compasses or GPS, but the peoples of the South Sea islands can build boats by hand, propel them by paddle, and navigate by watching the stars and weather patterns. By using these ancient methods, they can travel from island to

10. *Homily 20 on Ephesians;* trans. Roth, *St. John Chrysostom,* 44.

island when gasoline has run out and the motorboats must stay in the harbor. They have learned things from Western culture, but Westerners can learn from them about how another culture lives harmoniously with the earth. Through learning, sharing, and mutual respect, diverse people can be drawn together in a unity that strengthens everyone and embraces their differences without dissolving them.

When diverse people follow the pattern of the Father, Son, and Holy Spirit—who live as equals and share all they are with each other—diversity can enrich everybody. It need not cause divisions and conflicts. Yet it takes intentional effort to avoid such divisiveness. In monastic communities, the monks or nuns work hard to live in harmony.

Basil of Caesarea was a guide to monastics in fourth-century Cappadocia. He taught his monks and nuns the importance of living in community instead of living alone as hermits. To explain why, he says that it is natural for human beings to live together. "Who," he asks, "does not know that the human being is a tame and communal animal, and is neither solitary nor savage? For nothing is so proper to our nature as to share our lives with each other, and to need each other, and to love our own kind."[11] Basil then explains that it is appropriate for God to command us to love our neighbors, since he has made it natural for us to do so.

Love for neighbor is a primary task for all Christians, as it was in particular for Basil's monastics. This is why he strongly urges them to live in community. In *Long Rules* 7, he gives many reasons why he prefers communal life to life alone. The first reason is basic human need: "No one of us is self-sufficient for our own bodily needs, but in the procurement of necessities we need each other." Further, community life enables us to care for the needs of others, not only for our own needs. It gives us an opportunity to serve and keeps us from being self-absorbed. In addition, when we take a wrong turn in life, there is someone to set us right. Otherwise, we could remain on the wrong road

---

11. *Long Rules* 3; trans. Harrison, *St. Basil*, 117.

until we get in a wreck. Moreover, God has asked his people to do many kinds of good deeds, and one person alone cannot do them all. While doing one, he is unable to do another. "For example," Basil observes, "when visiting the sick one cannot welcome the stranger."[12] Yet a community has the resources to do both simultaneously.

Doing good works such as these and others is enabled by the Holy Spirit, who gives different gifts to different people. The Spirit, indeed, is a source of positive human diversity and individuality (see 1 Cor. 12:4–11). Yet in community life, Basil says, "the gift proper to each becomes common to all those living together." The gift received by one monk is equally received by his brothers, since the Holy Spirit has given it for the sake of all of them, not just one. The gifted brother has the task of working with the Spirit to share his gift with the whole community.[13] Thus those who live together benefit from the gifts bestowed on each. So each receives many gifts in community, not only the one bestowed on oneself. This abundance can bring strength and joy to all alike.

If marriage can be an image of the Trinity, as Chrysostom says, so can other forms of human community, beginning with monasticism. The famous Russian icon of the Trinity mentioned in chapter 8 was painted by Andrei Rublev, a monk in a community that had been founded by Sergius of Radonezh and had been dedicated to the Holy Trinity. Sergius, like Basil, was the founder of many monasteries and was the inspiration of monastic life across an entire country. Sergius named his main community after the Trinity because he saw the divine life as a model for his brothers' life together. Rublev, a disciple of Sergius, painted for his brothers an icon of the Trinity to which their monastery was dedicated. Yet at the same time it was an image of the community life he knew, for the brothers in their life together were themselves a living icon of the Holy Trinity.[14]

12. *Long Rules* 7.1; trans. Harrison, *St. Basil*, 119–20.

13. *Long Rules* 7.3; trans. Harrison, *St. Basil*, 121.

14. Gabriel Bunge, *The Rublev Trinity*, trans. Andrew Louth (Crestwood, NY: St. Vladimir's Seminary Press, 2007). This book contains fine reproductions of the icon.

The community Basil founded is an image of the Holy Trinity too, though it was portrayed by a living group of human beings and not, as far as we know, with paint on wood.

Creativity and Exchange

The shared life of a monastery is also a microcosm of sharing in human society on a larger scale. Theodoret of Cyrus, who lived in the fifth century, provides an insightful analysis of creativity as it is manifest in human societies and cultures. He speaks of human creativity as an image of God's creativity:

> In imitation of God who has created, the human being also fashions houses, walls, cities, harbors, ships, dockyards, chariots, and countless other things. On them there are depictions of the sky, sun, moon and stars, pictures of human beings and images of nonrational animals. Yet the difference in [modes of] fashioning is infinite. For on the one hand God fashions all things, both from things that exist and from things that do not exist, and apart from labor and time. For his expectation immediately brings into being what was planned. On the other hand, the human being needs matter and also tools, planning, reflection, time, labor, and other skills to produce what comes into being. For the builder needs the metal worker, and the metal worker [needs] the miner and the charcoal maker, and all alike need the woodcutter, the vine dresser, and the farmer. Thus each skill is assisted in a related task by the other skills. Yet indeed thus the human being in fashioning imitates to some extent the Creator, as an image imitates the archetype.[15]

Theodoret contrasts God's work of creation out of nothing, which God can produce instantly, and human creativity, which requires materials, training, tools, and time. Moreover, Theodoret takes into account what is today called art as well as the skills of craftsmanship, agriculture, and manufacturing.

---

15. *Questions on Genesis*; ed. Fernández Marcos and Sáenz-Badillos, *Theodoreti Cyrensis*, 25–26.

This patristic appreciation of multifaceted human creativity as included in the image of God could provide a good starting point for theological reflection about human civilization. In fact, it is a good commentary on our discussion of arts and sciences, the fruits of human culture, in chapter 8.

Theodoret finds a home in this chapter because the above passage also discusses human diversity and community. God can create by himself, or rather the Trinity creates, but humans need to work together to create things, and no one does so without the contributions of other people. The blacksmith needs wood and charcoal to heat the iron so he can fashion it into a horseshoe. He cannot work unless there are woodcutters and charcoal makers. All these workers need farmers to provide them with food. And indeed, the farmer's horses need shoes from the blacksmith.

Different people create many different things in abundantly diverse ways. Yet in human communities, the different things people make are shared and exchanged so as to benefit everybody. Theodoret describes the human interdependence and cooperation inherent in the division of labor. The Father, Son, and Holy Spirit are always sharing with each other; they share in their creative activities, and they exchange what they are. So even everyday economic activity, when done honestly and with good will toward others, can reveal the image of the Trinity.

The interchange of gifts and of labor also occurred in the Egyptian desert. Although they each lived alone or in small groups, the desert fathers and mothers, no less than Basil, were aware that they belonged to a monastic community, though it was not organized in the same way as the communities in Cappadocia. Let us recall the story at the end of chapter 6, in which John the Short allowed the distinguished priest to serve him a drink. John's discretion came from his understanding that the monks all belonged to a community, and they received, gave, and exchanged gifts. In fact, this is the condition of humankind in general. To receive, give, and exchange with love and thanksgiving is to act in the likeness of the Holy Trinity.

Leadership among Equals

Just as the Father, Son, and Holy Spirit are equal, all human persons made in their image are ultimately equal. The divine image confers dignity on each one. We discussed the implications of this statement in chapter 5. It means that the people who were despised in the late antique Mediterranean world, such as women, slaves, and lepers, were to be treated with care and respect. The same is true of all people today.

Yet there is also leadership in the Trinity. God the Father begets the Son and breathes forth the Holy Spirit. He gives each of them all that he is so that they are forever his equals. So while the Father exercises leadership in the Trinity, he is simultaneously the source of equality among the divine persons. He comes first, and the other two come with him. All that the Trinity does originates in the Father's good will and is accomplished through the Son in the Holy Spirit.[16] Human leadership that honors those who are led as equals is therefore a likeness of the Father. And human communities that are organized so as to balance leadership, equality, and harmonious collaboration bear the likeness of the Trinity.

The most effective leaders often lead by example. Vladimir Monomakh, a Russian prince who died in 1125, left this advice for his son and successor: "First of all, do not forget the poor; but in the measure of your possibilities feed them and make presents to the orphan; give justice to the widow and do not permit the mighty to ruin any man. . . . Visit the sick, walk behind the dead, for we are all mortal; do not pass a man without greeting, say a kind word to him."[17]

I imagine Prince Vladimir walking in a funeral procession behind the coffin. Behind him is a large group of his people, who follow him in mourning and honoring the departed. He calls his son to identify with those who are poor, sick, and even

16. Basil, *On the Holy Spirit* 18.47; Gregory of Nazianzus, *Oration* 38.9; Gregory of Nyssa, *On Not Three Gods.*

17. Russian chronicle quoted in George P. Fedotov, *The Russian Religious Mind*, 2 vols. (Belmont, MA: Nordland, 1975), 1:255.

dead. His task will be to rule them while remembering that they are his equals, to lead by setting an example, by going first and empowering them to come with him. This humility, this sense of community, makes a leader in the image of God the Father.

Humility in leadership is crucial. This means a clear, grounded, and truthful sense of one's own place in relationship to God and other people. In the eleventh century, Isiaslav, another Russian prince who lived far from the monastery, wanted to consult with the abbot Theodosius of the Kiev Caves, who was one of the founders of Russian and Ukrainian monasticism. The humble abbot, dressed in poor clothing with no insignia of office, came to Isiaslav's home for a visit and stayed until evening. Afterward the prince ordered that Theodosius be driven back to the monastery in his own coach so he could rest on the way. During the journey the coachman noticed his poor clothes and concluded that he was a beggar, so he said to him, "Look here, monk, you are free every day to do as you please, while I must spend my life in toil. Let me lie down in the coach, and you ride the horse." Theodosius, who led the brotherhood in doing lots of physical labor, humbly traded places with the driver. So they journeyed all night. As the abbot rode, he rejoiced and praised God. When he got sleepy he dismounted and walked to stay awake. In the morning, noblemen passing on the road recognized Theodosius and bowed to him, asking his blessing. The young coachman was dismayed to see the "beggar" receive such honor, and the abbot gently asked him to ride the horse again. When they reached the monastery, the coachman saw all the monks bowing to the ground to greet their abbot, and he was frightened and wondered who this great personage could be. Theodosius took him by the hand, brought him to the community dining hall, and ordered that he be given as much food and drink as he wanted. Then he paid him money and let him go.[18] While he remained respectful to everyone, the abbot completely disregarded social custom and class hierarchy and

18. George P. Fedotov, *A Treasury of Russian Spirituality* (New York: Harper, 1965), 33–34.

respected the personal dignity and need of the young, ignorant workman who was tired and needed to rest.[19]

Conclusion

With God's help, human communities are called to manifest the image of the Holy Trinity in a number of ways. People should live together in peace and love, with mutual respect. They should regard one another as equals, though in each situation some lead and others follow. They should maintain a balance between the way people are alike and the way each one is unique, then allow both the common human experience and the unique gifts of its members to strengthen the whole group. With community support, people should work creatively to produce things that others need, then share and exchange these goods with one another. Those with the requisite gifts should use their creativity to pursue the arts and sciences and share the results of their insights with the community as a whole.

There are many ways that communities can go wrong. People can behave like atomistic individuals, distancing themselves from others and refusing to care for them or accept their care. Governments can impose totalitarian conformity, reinforcing the ways people are alike while trying to stamp out their uniqueness. Leaders can establish unjust hierarchies, keeping their gifts to themselves and withholding them from others instead of sharing. Or communities can be torn apart by divisive conflicts. But if they preserve the balance summed up in the life of the Trinity and live in God's likeness, these pitfalls can be avoided. A community that follows the pattern of the Trinity by combining sameness and difference, giving and receiving, equality and servant leadership, mutual thanksgiving and respect will little by little transform its social structure toward peace and justice.

19. This paragraph is borrowed, with minor modifications, from Nonna Verna Harrison, "Leadership in the Orthodox Christian Tradition," in *Traditions in Leadership: How Faith Traditions Shape the Way We Lead*, ed. Richard J. Mouw and Eric O. Jacobsen (Pasadena, CA: De Pree Leadership Center, 2006), 93.

Conclusion

The angels keep their ancient places—
Turn but a stone and start a wing!
'Tis ye, 'tis your estrangèd faces,
That miss the many-splendored thing.[1]

This poem, "The Kingdom of God" by Francis Thompson, is where I found the term "many-splendored." His message is that although we cannot see it, at every point in this world the spiritual world is near. The two realms are superimposed on each other in the same space. So we can grasp spiritual realities if we stretch our perceptions, as he says in the first stanza:

O world invisible, we view thee,
O world intangible, we touch thee,
O world unknowable, we know thee,
Inapprehensible, we clutch thee![2]

Thus if I turn over a pebble in my garden, I may glimpse not a beetle but an angel that was hidden beneath it. But what might

1. http://theotherpages.org/poems/thomps01.html (accessed April 24, 2009).
2. http://theotherpages.org/poems/thomps01.html (accessed April 24, 2009).

I glimpse behind the face of my neighbor? The human, made in the image of God, is at least potentially very much like an angel. Together with the angels, humans are near to God and participate in the spiritual realm, for we are all called to worship God together. Yet we humans are also embodied and share the earth's ecosystem with calico cats, broad-winged condors, and red-leafed Japanese maple trees.

Early Christians had different opinions on whether angels were made in God's image. I rather hope they are and that as the Lord's faithful servants they can share in the full inheritance of saintly human beings when God's kingdom has fully come. In this prosaic age, surely we often miss the splendors of the angels' presence. But can we see the many splendors of God's image, and the potentialities of God's likeness, in the people with whom we spend our days and our lives?

Many Facets of the Divine Image

Let us review some of the splendors described in this book:

Chapter 1 shows how freedom and responsibility are gifts from God that constitute central facets of the divine image. God, who loves us, has given us freedom so that unlike robots or puppets we can love him in return. We choose what we do, what habits we cultivate, which cultural influences and role models we follow, and what we will become in the future. Like actors capable of playing different roles in the same play, we can take on the likeness of God, but we can choose the likeness of a savage beast instead, or even the likeness of a devil. Yet we are capable of choosing and doing good and have a responsibility to do so.

We remain free, although our freedom is limited. Yet we can take tiny positive steps that enable further tiny positive steps. Over time our bad habits and addictions can be overcome by God's grace, wise practical training, and our own sustained efforts. We are invited to work with God to co-create our future identity in a way that is more and more Christlike. When we follow this calling we also acquire more and more inner freedom.

As we grow spiritually, we become aware of our choices and opt for goodness instead of being driven by cultural influences, bad habits, or misguided impulses. The greatest freedom is loving God and neighbor spontaneously by discerning God's will and choosing it in every moment.

Chapter 2 is about how God is the foundation of our human existence and identity. God has fashioned us in his image so that he will always love us; so that we remain connected to him at the core of our being, regardless of whether we know it; and so that we are always capable of loving him in return. We fell by turning away from God, with devastating consequences. But Christ, who always remains God, assumed human nature in order to mend the divine image in us and bring us back to our Creator.

Chapter 3 is about spiritual perception and relationship. To love God and our neighbors as God intends, we have to know them truly. An important facet of the divine image is the capacity to perceive God and our neighbors as spiritual beings. Yet we are often unaware of this capacity, and our perceptions are often distorted. But our buried capacities for authentic spiritual perception can be restored through the divine gift of revelation and can grow throughout a lifetime of sanctification. Such perception brings practical wisdom. It enables deeply loving service to neighbors and to God's creation even in the face of seemingly insurmountable obstacles.

Chapter 4 is about virtues and emotions. It asks, "Can I really do good?" People who have turned from crime or self-destruction and have become leaders in loving, creative service to God and neighbor show that it can be done. Because we bear the image of God, we are all capable of virtue, and in principle all are called to become saints. The real question, though, is how such positive transformation can be sustained despite a lifetime of obstacles and challenges. Can ordinary human beings like us, beset by countless problems, weaknesses, and dangers, follow the paths trod by the saints and heroes we have known in our families and communities and whose testimonies and examples have illumined humankind throughout history? Even if we can only walk the paths of virtue for a short distance, this can make a genuine difference in our own lives and the lives of others. Small acts of kindness, truthfulness, and justice, repeated over time, can have an enormous cumulative effect. With continual help from God, authentic virtues like perseverance, moderation, and generosity can truly be learned and put into practice one moment at a time.

Virtues are originally aspects of God's own character and way of acting. They compose the most important dimension of the divine likeness for which every human being is called: we are to love as God loves. As persons made in God's image, we are invited by grace to participate in God's virtues, such as justice, wisdom, humility, compassion, and above all love. Yet mature love comes at the end of a long growth process, not at the beginning. As we struggle toward virtue and sanctification, our bad habits, negative obsessions, and misdirected emotions can be slowly reoriented so that we arrive at a harmonious wholeness. Then the tremendous energies bound within our minds and emotions can be poured forth freely as love and service to God and neighbor. And above all, we need the virtue of humility to keep us grounded and open to help and guidance from God and from other people.

We saw in chapter 5 that as bearers of the divine image human persons are intrinsically endowed with royal dignity. Yet this is not a dignity that exalts some people over others, for it belongs equally to all who are human, and it is not primarily about power or sovereignty. Rather, it is a gift from the Creator, the intrinsic value, honor, and splendor of the children of God that lies hidden at the inmost core of every human being. Early Christians prophetically challenged Roman ideas of social class by affirming that royal dignity belongs to everyone and is not based on such factors as the world's wealth, health, social status, or political power, all of which are transitory. Leading Christian theologians declared that the divine image belongs equally to men and women, rich and poor, and includes social outcasts such as the many slaves of the ancient world and the homeless disabled. It follows that all are entitled to care and respect. The same is true today, in a world where there are many abused children, victims of torture, and even slaves. These people are treated as objects of shame rather than objects of dignity. Sometimes systematic efforts are made to erase their memory that they have authentic value and freedom as human persons. Such crimes are also crimes against God, whose image these people bear. The perpetrators oppose everything that is affirmed in this book. Their evil actions must be opposed.

Chapter 6 is about human embodiment. Early Christians strongly affirmed that the human body is good and has an essential part in the work of the divine image. Through our bodies we serve God and give, receive, and share life with our neighbors. When the soul, mind, and heart turn toward God, the body also is turned toward God, becomes the soul's honored collaborator, and comes to be filled with divine life.

Chapter 7 is about how all human beings, as God's image, are called to a royal priesthood. Our bodies make essential contributions to this ministry. It is our God-given responsibility both to gather the praise and thankfulness of all creation and offer it to God and to bring God's blessing to all creation. Early Christians believed that human beings can mediate between God and the natural world because we participate in every level of creation. As contemporary scientists have also discovered, we are interconnected with every living creature in earth's biosphere and every object in the physical universe. Ancient and modern saints have disclosed how people can collaborate with God to bring about the harmony and flourishing of the world's creatures. Human sovereignty over the earth has been abused and discredited, but the present condition of the earth's environment shows that human responsibility is inescapable. People today have the task of learning more fully how the earth's natural systems work so as to care for them wisely and with love.

Chapter 8 is about how human reason, creativity, and culture can manifest the divine image and likeness. Early Christians believed that our reason participates in God's reason and that our creativity is an image of divine creativity. As they measure and map and describe how God has created parts of the universe, some of the greatest scientists in modern times have rediscovered for themselves the link between human reason and divine reason. Science depends on the human capacities for perception, reason, and communication with others, all of which are the gifts of the divine image. The arts too perceive beauty in God's world and find ways to portray it and communicate it to others. Creativity and culture can thus be expressions of the divine image in humankind. Like the other gifts of the divine image, they too can be misused to turn people away from God. People can invent their own worlds in which God has no place, yet in the end they risk incorporating human sinfulness; in any case, they can never be as splendid as the world God has created. But the same gifts of culture and creativity can also be used to bring us to God through the wonders and beauties of his creation.

Chapter 9 is about human community. It asks what is distinctive about each human person and what all people have in common that binds them together. The mothers and fathers of the ancient desert recognized that there are many virtues, many gifts, and many ways of life that bring people to salvation. The Creator invites each person to follow a distinctive path uniquely suited to that person. Yet there are numerous gifts, needs, experiences, and responsibilities that all people share in common because all alike are human. Through our uniqueness and through all we have in common, humans are profoundly interconnected with one another. To be human is to be a unique individual and to be in community at the same time, just as the divine Trinity is three distinct persons in one essence. When people live together in the likeness of the Trinity, as far as is humanly possible, they hold in balance likeness and difference, harmony and mutual respect, giving and receiving, equality and leadership; in this way justice can flourish. Then diversity strengthens community while community enables diversity to flourish.

Christ as the Image of God

The stories of Adam and Eve show the kinship that all human beings share in common, demonstrating that we are all connected with one another through our humanity. And yet our human existence and the community we share are flawed by sin. So when the Son of God, the second person of the Trinity, made human nature his own and was born as Jesus Christ, he became the new and last Adam. So he has become the perfect manifestation of the divine image that defines humankind as human. Athanasius says that through his incarnation, Christ becomes the model who sits for the restoration of the divine image damaged by sin, yet as the Creator he is also the painter of God's image.[3] This means that Christ, who is God's perfect image, shares that image with humankind, thus restoring humankind to kinship with God and bringing it salvation from fallenness and sin.

Because he has become human, he has made all human persons his kin. He has become the origin and center of a new humankind, a new community. In Matthew 25:31–40 (NRSV), Christ shows what this means:

> When the Son of Man comes in his glory, and all the angels with him, then he will sit on the throne of his glory. All the nations will be gathered before him, and he will separate people one from another as a shepherd separates the sheep from the goats, and he will put the sheep at his right hand and the goats at the left. Then the king will say to those at his right hand, "Come, you that are blessed by my Father, inherit the kingdom prepared for you from the foundation of the world; for I was hungry and you gave me food, I was thirsty and you gave me something to drink, I was a stranger and you welcomed me, I was naked and you gave me clothing, I was sick and you took care of me, I was in prison and you visited me." Then the righteous will answer him, "Lord, when was it that we saw you hungry and gave you food, or thirsty and gave you something to drink? And when was it that we saw you a stranger and welcomed you, or naked and gave you clothing? And when was it that we saw you sick or in prison and visited you?" And the king will answer them, "Truly I tell you, just as you did it to one of the least of these who are members of my family, you did it to me."

3. *On the Incarnation* 14.1–2.

Of course, the king in this story, the Son of Man, is Christ himself. He identifies himself first of all with the poor, those who lack basic necessities like food, drink, clothing, and shelter. He dwells in them, so that those who serve them are actually serving him. Though they have borne great shame in human society, he shares with them his immeasurable dignity. In this way, he restores to them the royalty of the image of God, which we discussed in chapter 5. Surely, Christ's act of identification and union with them includes all who were marginalized in ancient society, such as women, the disabled, the homeless, and slaves; it includes all who are marginalized today. Astonishingly, in the story he does not ask them to do anything to merit such union with him. He simply loves them and counts them as his own family. He does not even have to say that they are blessed by the Father and will inherit the kingdom prepared for them since before the world's creation. This reality is already established, and he takes it as given.

The audience he addresses directly is composed of people who do have food, drink, clothing, and shelter, who are not limited by illness or imprisonment but are free to visit and help those who are. He asks those who love him, the Son of God, to love their neighbors also and to demonstrate their love in action. This ties in with what we discussed in chapter 4: deeds of virtue, or righteousness, establish the divine likeness in a person. Virtues, which have their source and fulfillment in Christ, unite a person with Christ, make that person a member of Christ's family, and bring all the righteous, with the poor, to God's kingdom.

Notice also that the story Christ tells is about bodily needs and bodily assistance. Here people's bodies play a central role in God's image and likeness (chapter 6). This approach must have come naturally to Christ, because he assumed a human body and united it with God.

By telling this story, Christ also encourages people to stretch their spiritual senses, to see him in their neighbors, and to act in such a way that their neighbors can see him in them. Thus he takes the lead in re-establishing the spiritual perception that is a facet of the divine image, as discussed in chapter 3. By seeing

Christ as God incarnate, we can learn to see our fellow human beings truly, for they are God's image.

This story depicts humankind as united in community, a topic we discussed in chapter 9. In this life, basic human needs and the giving and receiving through which they are met reveal Christ's presence and establish the divine likeness in humankind. By such giving and receiving together with Christ, people are preparing themselves and each other for the community life of the kingdom God has planned since before the world's creation, a kingdom in which all will be joined with Christ and with one another as members of one family. The head of that family is no longer Adam but Christ.

We have seen throughout this book that the fulfillment of the divine image in humankind is communion with God, so as to know him and be known by him. It is sharing in his eternal life so that we can be freed from death. It is dwelling in him as he dwells in us. It is choosing and doing what God wills and chooses so that we can share with him in his loving and creative activities. It is participation in Christ, which enables imitation of Christ. Christ is the vine, we are the branches (see John 15:5). He shared our human life so that we, by his grace, can share his divine life. In other words, he became human to enable humans to become divine. Although until now I have not used this word, because it can easily be misunderstood, the goal of the divine image—the purpose for which God created it—is *theōsis*, the divinization of humankind.

This does *not* mean what the serpent said when he told Eve that she and Adam would "be like God" apart from God (see Gen. 3:5). Yet that lie was effective because it was so close to the truth. The purpose of human existence *is* to become godlike, for we were created in God's likeness with the task of manifesting it more and more. Yet the only source of real divine life is God himself. Real human godlikeness must therefore be derived entirely from God. So the only way humans can share in divine life is by staying close to God, united with God, choosing what God chooses, doing along with God what God is doing first—and such activity is always grounded in love. It is not prideful or self-serving. It does not come through disobeying God and thus moving away from him, as Adam and Eve did in the garden. Yet God has come to us in Christ as human in order to unite us with God's self again after our fall.

The Image of Divine Mystery

This book describes many ways in which human persons and communities can embody and manifest God's image and likeness. Yet we can never claim to include everything there is to say on the subject. As Gregory of Nyssa says, human identity is an unfathomable depth of mystery, which is itself an image of the inexhaustible and boundless mystery of the divine being and life.[4] This means that the divine image at the core of what we are as human remains multifaceted and is open to transformation in a future that is now unknown to us. However much we may come to know of God and of human existence, there is always more waiting to be discovered and a further mystery that remains beyond our grasp. We are on a journey of discovery that has no end.

To live according to God's image and likeness in the ways this book describes is to be truly alive. And we can dare to hope to become more fully alive in ways that we cannot now imagine. The human likeness to God is participation in God's life and immortality; it is abundant new life here and now and eternal life with God in the age to come.

---

4. *On the Creation of Humanity* 11.2–4; trans. Moore and Wilson, *Gregory*, 396–97.

Select Bibliography

Texts

Bernardi, Jean, ed. *Grégoire de Nazianze: Discours 1–3*. Sources chrétiennes 247. Paris: Cerf, 1978.

Butler, Edward Cuthbert. *The Lausiac History of Palladius: A Critical Discussion together with Notes on Early Egyptian Monasticism.* Texts and Studies 6. Cambridge: Cambridge University Press, 1904.

Calvet-Sebasti, Marie-Ange, ed. *Grégoire de Nazianze: Discours 6–12.* Sources chrétiennes 405. Paris: Cerf, 1995.

Courtonne, Yves, ed. *Saint Basile: Lettres.* 3 vols. Paris: Les Belles Lettres, 1957–66.

Cross, Frank Leslie, ed. *Athanasius, De Incarnatione: An Edition of the Greek Text.* London: SPCK, 1939.

Crouzel, Henri, and Manlio Simonetti, eds. *Origène: Traité des principes.* Sources chrétiennes 252–53, 268–69, 312. Paris: Cerf, 1978–84.

Descourtieux, Patrick, ed. *Clément d'Alexandrie: Stromate VI.* Sources chrétiennes 446. Paris: Cerf, 1999.

Fernández Marcos, Natalio, and Angel Sáenz-Badillos, eds. *Theodoreti Cyrensis Quaestiones in Octateuchum: Editio Critica.* Madrid: Textos y Estudios Cardinal Cisneros de la Biblia Poliglota Matritense, 1979.

Guillaumont, Antoine, and Claire Guillaumont, eds. *Evagre le Pontique: Traité pratique, ou, Le moine*. Sources chrétiennes 170–71. Paris: Cerf, 1971.

Heck, Arie van, ed. *Gregorii Nysseni De pauperibus amandis: Orationes duo*. Leiden: Brill, 1964.

Jaeger, Werner, ed. *Gregorii Nysseni Opera*. 9 vols. Leiden: Brill, 1960–. Cited as GNO.

Kotter, Bonifatius, ed. *Die Schriften des Johannes von Damaskos*. 5 vols. Patristische Texte und Studien 7, 12, 17, 22, 29. Berlin: Walter de Gruyter, 1969–88.

Marcovich, Miroslav, ed. *Contra Celsum, Libri VIII Origenis*. Vigiliae Christianae supplement 54. Leiden: Brill, 2001.

Marcovich, M., ed. *Clementis Alexandrini Paedagogus*. Leiden: Brill, 2002.

Marrou, Henri-Irénée, ed. *Clément d'Alexandrie: Le pédagogue*, vol. 1. Sources chrétiennes 70. Paris: Cerf, 1960.

Migne, J. P., ed. *Patrologia Graeca*. Cited as PG; a good source for editions not cited elsewhere.

Moreschini, Claudio, ed. *Grégoire de Nazianze: Discours 38–41*. Sources chrétiennes 358. Paris: Cerf, 1990.

Petruccione, John F., and Robert C. Hill, eds. *The Questions on the Octateuch, Theodoret of Cyrus*. Library of Early Christianity 1, 2. Washington, DC: Catholic University of America Press, 2007.

Petschenig, Michael, and Eugene Pichery, ed. *Jean Cassien: Conférences*. Sources chrétiennes 42 bis. Paris: Cerf, 2008.

Regnault, Lucien, and Jacques de Préville, eds. *Dorothée de Gaza: Oeuvres spirituelles*. Sources chrétiennes 92. Paris: Cerf, 1963.

Rudberg, Stig Y. *L'homélie de Basile de Césarée sur le mot, "Ovserve-toi toi-même."* Acta Universitatis Stockholmiensis, Studia Graeca Stockholmiensia 2. Stockholm: Almqvist & Wiksell, 1962.

Sagnard, F., Adelin Rousseau, and Louis Doutreleau, eds. *Irénée de Lyon: Contre les hérésies*. Sources chrétiennes 34, 100, 152–53, 210–11, 263–64, 293–94. Paris: Cerf, 1952–82.

Smets, Alexis, and Michel van Esbroeck, eds. *Basile de Césarée: Sur l'origine de l'homme*. Sources chrétiennes 160. Paris: Cerf, 1970.

Translations

Please note that I have often modified published translations and noted these modifications by adding "alt." to the footnote. These may be minor alterations, such as the replacement of one or two words, but in a few cases I have reworked the whole passage from the Greek text. My reasons for making changes vary. Sometimes it is done for the sake of inclusive language, in accord with contemporary English usage, such as changing "man" to "the human." Sometimes altering a word or two can improve clarity. More extensive changes in language are intended to make difficult texts accessible to contemporary readers without changing their meanings. Often this simply means breaking up long sentences and adjusting word order, but at times more retranslation is needed. This is particularly necessary when existing translations were made in the nineteenth century. In some cases, I have replaced a translation and cited the text's Greek edition. However, to encourage further reading, published translations of early Christian sources discussed in this book are listed here.

Anonymous [a religious of CSMV], trans. *St. Athanasius on the Incarnation.* Popular Patristics Series. Crestwood, NY: St. Vladimir's Seminary Press, 1996.

Bamberger, John Eudes, trans. *Evagrius Ponticus: The Praktikos; Chapters on Prayer.* Cistercian Studies 4. Kalamazoo, MI: Cistercian, 1978.

Behr, John, trans. *St. Irenaeus of Lyons: On the Apostolic Preaching.* Popular Patristics Series. Crestwood, NY: St. Vladimir's Seminary Press, 1997.

Butterworth, G. W., trans. *Origen on First Principles.* Gloucester, MA: Peter Smith, 1973.

Callahan, Virginia Woods, trans. *Saint Gregory of Nyssa: Ascetical Works.* Fathers of the Church 58. Washington, DC: Catholic University of America Press, 1967.

Chadwick, Henry, trans. *Origen: Contra Celsum.* Cambridge: Cambridge University Press, 1953.

Daley, Brian E., trans. *Gregory of Nazianzus*. The Early Church Fathers. London and New York: Routledge, 2006.

Hall, Stuart G., trans. "Gregory of Nyssa, *On the Beatitudes*." In *Gregory of Nyssa: Homilies on the Beatitudes: An English Version with Commentary and Supporting Studies*, edited by Hubertus R. Drobner and Albert Viciano, 21–90. Leiden: Brill, 2000.

Harrison, Nonna Verna, trans. *St. Basil the Great on the Human Condition*. Popular Patristics Series. Crestwood, NY: St. Vladimir's Seminary Press, 2005.

————, trans. *St. Gregory of Nazianzus: Festal Orations*. Popular Patristics Series. Crestwood, NY: St. Vladimir's Seminary Press, 2008.

Hill, Robert Charles, trans. *Theodoret of Cyrus: The Questions on the Octateuch*. Vol. 1, *On Genesis and Exodus*. Library of Early Christianity. Washington, DC: Catholic University of America Press, 2007.

Louth, Andrew, trans. *John of Damascus: Three Treatises on the Divine Images*. Popular Patristics Series. Crestwood, NY: St. Vladimir's Seminary Press, 2003.

————, trans. *Maximus the Confessor*. The Early Church Fathers. London and New York: Routledge, 1996.

Luibheid, Colm, trans. *John Cassian: Conferences*. Classics of Western Spirituality. New York: Paulist Press, 1985.

Malherbe, Abraham J., and Everett Ferguson, trans. *Gregory of Nyssa: The Life of Moses*. Classics of Western Spirituality. New York: Paulist Press, 1978.

Meyer, Robert T., trans. *Palladius: The Lausiac History*. Ancient Christian Writers 34. Westminster, MD: Newman, 1965.

Moore, William, and Henry Austin Wilson, trans. *Select Writings and Letters of Gregory, Bishop of Nyssa*, Nicene and Post-Nicene Fathers 2, vol. 5. Grand Rapids: Eerdmans, 1979. This volume contains *On the Making of Man* and *On Infants' Early Deaths*. I have retranslated the first of these titles as *On the Creation of Humanity*.

Ramsey, Boniface, trans. *John Cassian: The Conferences*. Ancient Christian Writers 57. New York: Paulist Press, 1997.

Roberts, Alexander, and James Donaldson, trans. *The Writings of the Fathers Down to A.D. 325*, Ante-Nicene Fathers, vol. 2. Grand

Rapids: Eerdmans, 1986. Contains Clement of Alexandria, *Stromata* (*Miscellanies*). Cited as ANF 2.

Roth, Catharine P., trans. *St. Gregory of Nyssa: On the Soul and the Resurrection.* Popular Patristics Series. Crestwood, NY: St. Vladimir's Seminary Press, 1993.

———, trans. *St. John Chrysostom: On Wealth and Poverty.* Popular Patristics Series. Crestwood, NY: St. Vladimir's Seminary Press, 1984.

Saward, John, trans. *The Scandal of the Incarnation: Irenaeus Against the Heresies.* San Francisco: Ignatius, 1990.

Sinkewicz, Robert E., trans. *Evagrius of Pontus: The Greek Ascetic Corpus.* Oxford: Oxford University Press, 2003.

Vinson, Martha, trans. *St. Gregory of Nazianzus: Select Orations.* Fathers of the Church 107. Washington, DC: Catholic University of America Press, 2003.

Ward, Benedicta, trans. *The Desert Fathers: Sayings of the Early Christian Monks.* London: Penguin, 2003. Cited as *Desert Fathers.*

———, trans. *The Sayings of the Desert Fathers: The Alphabetical Collection.* Rev. ed. Cistercian Studies 59. Kalamazoo, MI: Cistercian, 1975. Cited as *Sayings.*

Wheeler, Eric P., trans. *Dorotheos of Gaza: Discourses and Sayings.* Cistercian Studies 33. Kalamazoo, MI: Cistercian, 1977.

Wood, Simon P., trans. *Clement of Alexandria: Christ the Educator.* Fathers of the Church 23. Washington, DC: Catholic University of America Press, 1954.

Index